orange almond cake

ready in 50 minutes | serves 8 or more

I love this cake drizzled with a tangy fruit syrup such as passionfruit and lime, but it's also good with berry fruits and cream or ice cream, or try it with the exotic fruit salad on page 80.

100g unsalted butter, cubed and softened

100g caster sugar

2 small (size 5) free-range eggs, at room temperature

170g fine semolina

70g ground almonds

2 tsp baking powder

50ml freshly squeezed orange juice

for serving

icing sugar, for dusting

fruit syrup or fruit salad of your choice

vanilla ice cream or plain yoghurt (optional)

1 Preheat oven to 180°C (regular bake). Line the base of a 20cm cake tin with baking paper.

2 Put butter in a bowl and beat briefly with an electric beater until creamy and loose. Beat in caster sugar in three lots, and beat until fluffy and lighter in colour (creamed; see cooking class on page 111). You'll need to stop the machine and scrape down the sides of the bowl several times. Break eggs into a small dish and beat lightly with a fork. Add eggs gradually, beating well after each addition, and adding up to 3 tablespoons of semolina to help stabilise the mixture. With a large spoon mix in almonds, remaining semolina, baking powder and, lastly, the orange juice.

3 Turn cake batter into prepared tin and smooth the top with a knife. Bake for 25–30 minutes, or until a skewer inserted into the centre of the cake comes out clean. Cool for 10 minutes in the cake tin, then turn out onto a cooling rack. Transfer to a serving plate when cool.

4 Dust with icing sugar and serve cut into wedges drizzled with fruit syrup or fruit salad, and with dollops of vanilla ice cream or yoghurt alongside if liked.

Taste
sweet feast

Taste sweet feast

Julie Biuso

photography by Aaron McLean

NEW HOLLAND

First published in 2011 by
New Holland Publishers (NZ) Ltd
Auckland • Sydney • London • Cape Town
www.newhollandpublishers.co.nz

218 Lake Road, Northcote, Auckland 0627,
New Zealand
Unit 1, 66 Gibbes Street, Chatswood, NSW
2067, Australia
86–88 Edgware Road, London W2 2EA,
United Kingdom
80 McKenzie Street, Cape Town 8001,
South Africa

ISBN: 978 1 86966 335 3

Commissioned by Belinda Cooke
Publishing manager: Christine Thomson
Editor: Teresa McIntyre
Design: Christine Hansen

A catalogue record for this book is
available from the National Library
of New Zealand.

10 9 8 7 6 5 4 3 2 1

Colour reproduction by Image Centre Ltd.,
Auckland
Printed in China through Phoenix Offset,
Hong Kong, on paper sourced from
sustainable forests.

contents

introduction

Over the years I have put hundreds of sweet recipes into print. I draw my inspiration from my mother, because – while she was a great cook of all sorts of dishes – it was in cake-making and sweet things that she excelled. Our house was never without a tin full of deliciousness: something sweet, crunchy, nutty or chocolatey to chew on. Tuesdays and Thursdays were her baking days. We'd round the corner of our house after school to be greeted by an overwhelming smell of sweet browning butter and sugar, toasted nuts and coconut, chocolate and spice. The only advantage I recall about being the youngest of a large family was that I got home from school first, sometimes in time to help blow the shells off roasted peanuts, lick the bowl for a treat, or transfer biscuits to a cooling rack, spurred on to help by imagining in my mind eating everything up before the others got home.

Traditions ought to be carried on, more so now than ever in this fast-changing world. My own daughter used to walk in from kindergarten, sniff the air and ask, 'Whadaya cookin' mamma?'; a simple question, perhaps, but one loaded with hope, longing and expectation, which quickly became bound up with love. Somehow, through baking, we can show we care for someone in a way which seems more tangible than just cooking the evening meal.

Memories of baking are evocative, powerful, sustaining, nourishing. Every time I peel a Granny Smith apple, cut it and sprinkle it with sugar, and sniff that sweet green apple scent, my mother is with me. I am in her kitchen and she's preparing an apple pie – I am sneaking slices of apple off the chopping board under her watchful eye; she's telling me not to but her eyes are twinkling. The smell is so locked in my memory that I have to focus to bring myself back to the reality of my own kitchen in the present.

This collection of recipes is special because they are my favourites from *Taste* magazine, including several my mother used to make. When I flip back over past issues and see the sweet recipes I have cooked, I get excited about them all over again because here are cakes, tarts and pies, crumbles, puddings, desserts and sweet things I've shared with my family and friends over the years, everyday stuff mingled with the stuff of dreams. It's as if every recipe tells a story: a cake baked for a birthday, a summer tart quickly assembled to use up seasonal fruit which then became a family classic, a mid-winter steamed pud which filled the hunger gaps so well leaving us all replete and content, and a Christmas cake, all the family gathered in the kitchen, hands on the long-handled wooden spoon, stirring and making a wish.

I hope you enjoy the recipes, too; and, if you are just starting off in the kitchen, that there is enough inspiration and practical information in this book to inspire you to start your own baking traditions.

Special thanks to Suzanne Dale, Editor of *Taste*, and her team at the magazine, Belinda Cooke and her team at New Holland, Teresa McIntyre for excellent editing, Christine Hansen for clever design; and to Aaron McLean for his superb photography and Julie Wyatt who did most of the prop styling for the photographs. Finally, thanks to Mary-Jane Mumford and Wendy Muir at Milly's, Auckland (www.millyskitchen.co.nz).

Julie Biuso
www.juliebiuso.com

cakes and sponges

blackberry cake

ready in 1 hour 10 minutes, plus cooling | serves 8

Blackberries give this tender-crusted cake plenty of flavour. If serving for dessert, accompany with a bowl of sugared blackberries and a bowl of Greek yoghurt or crème fraîche.

1 Preheat oven to 180°C (regular bake). Line the base and sides of a 23cm round cake tin with baking paper.

2 Put butter in a bowl and briefly beat with an electric beater until creamy and loose. Beat in caster sugar a tablespoon at a time and continue beating until fluffy and lighter in colour (creamed; see cooking class on page 30). You'll need to stop the machine and scrape down the sides of the bowl several times. Blend in vanilla extract. Lightly beat eggs together with a fork, then add them gradually to the creamed butter and sugar, adding 1–2 tablespoons of the measured flour about halfway through to help stabilise the mixture.

3 Sift the remaining flour and the baking powder together onto a piece of paper, then sift one-third of it over the creamed ingredients and fold in with a large spoon. Sift over and mix in another third of dry ingredients, then mix in the milk, and finally the last measure of dry ingredients.

4 Spoon mixture into prepared tin and smooth the top with a knife. Press blackberries into the cake batter, then sprinkle the top with cinnamon sugar.

5 Bake for about 50 minutes, until shrinking slightly from the sides of the tin and golden brown on top. Cool in the tin for 15 minutes, then turn out onto a plate lined with baking paper. Peel paper off bottom of cake if still attached, cover cake with a cooling rack, flip and lift off paper and plate. Serve warmish, dusted with icing sugar.

125g unsalted butter, cubed and softened
125g caster sugar
1 tsp vanilla extract
3 medium (size 6) free-range eggs, at room temperature
200g standard flour
2 tsp baking powder
2 Tbsp milk, at room temperature
300g blackberries
cinnamon sugar (mix 1 Tbsp caster sugar and ¼ tsp ground cinnamon)
icing sugar, for dusting

plum and almond cake

ready in 1 hour 15 minutes, plus cooling | serves 8 or more

Plums and almonds make great mates in this cake, which is surprisingly light. It will keep for several days.

200g unsalted butter, cubed and
    softened
225g caster sugar
4 medium (size 6) free-range eggs,
    at room temperature
150g self-raising flour, sifted
70g ground almonds
finely grated zest of 1 lemon
2 Tbsp milk, at room temperature
6 large plums (500g), washed
    and dried
icing sugar, for dusting

1 Preheat oven to 180°C (regular bake). Brush a 21cm cake tin with melted butter, put a disc of baking paper in the base, then shake a little flour around the tin (it will stick to the buttered sides). Tap out excess flour.

2 Put butter in a bowl and briefly beat with an electric beater until creamy and loose. Beat in caster sugar a tablespoon at a time and continue beating until fluffy and lighter in colour (creamed; see cooking class on page 111), stopping the machine and scraping down the sides of the bowl several times. Beat eggs together with a fork, then add them gradually to the creamed butter and sugar, adding 2 tablespoons of the measured flour halfway through beating to help stabilise the mixture.

3 Sift over remaining flour and fold in using a large metal spoon. Mix in the ground almonds, lemon zest and milk. Spoon cake batter into prepared tin, smoothing the top with a knife.

4 Halve the plums, remove stones and cut each half into 3–4 pieces. Place plums on top of cake batter – they don't need to be arranged as they will sink into the batter during cooking. Bake cake for 50–60 minutes, or until well risen and golden. The cake should spring back when touched with the finger and be shrinking slightly from the sides of the tin.

5 Remove cake from oven and let it cool for 15 minutes in the tin. Loosen from sides of tin with a flat-bladed knife. Turn cake out of tin by covering it with a large plate, then turning cake and plate over so cake falls onto plate. Lift tin off. Peel baking paper off bottom of cake if still attached, then cover cake with a cooling rack, flip over and lift off the plate. Leave to cool. Dust with icing sugar and transfer to a serving plate.

cinnamon apple cake

ready in 1 hour 15 minutes | serves 8 or more

Cinnamon and apple together is a crowd pleaser – try this cake for a special afternoon tea, or served warm for dessert with dollops of lightly whipped cream.

90g unsalted butter, cubed and
   softened

110g caster sugar

2 small (size 5) free-range eggs, at
   room temperature

175g self-raising flour

finely grated zest and juice of
   1 lemon

100ml milk, at room temperature

800g (about 4 large) Granny Smith
   or Braeburn apples

¼ tsp ground cinnamon

icing sugar, for dusting

1 Preheat oven to 180°C (regular bake). Line the base and sides of a 23cm cake tin with baking paper. Set aside 1 tablespoon of the measured caster sugar for the top of the cake.

2 Put butter in a bowl and briefly beat with an electric beater until creamy and loose. Beat in caster sugar a tablespoon at a time and continue beating until fluffy and lighter in colour (creamed; see cooking class on page 111), stopping the machine and scraping down the sides of the bowl several times. Beat eggs together with a fork, then add them gradually to the creamed butter and sugar, adding 1–2 tablespoons of the measured flour halfway through beating to help stabilise the mixture. Add the lemon zest.

3 Sift over one-third of the remaining flour and fold in, then add one-third of the milk. Repeat twice more and mix gently until just smooth. Transfer to prepared tin and carefully spread level with a flat-bladed knife.

4 Peel, quarter and core the apples, squeezing a little lemon juice over as they are prepared, to stop them going brown. Partially slice the pieces of apple, about three-quarters of the way through each piece, open them up like fans and press them deeply into the cake batter.

5 Mix the reserved tablespoon of sugar with the cinnamon and sprinkle on top of the cake. Bake for about 1 hour, until golden brown on top and slightly shrinking from the sides of the tin, and a skewer inserted into the centre of the cake comes out clean. Cool in the tin for 15 minutes. Turn the cake out of the tin by covering it with a large dinner plate, then turning cake and plate over and flopping cake onto plate. Lift off tin and peel off paper if still attached. Quickly put another plate on top (don't squash!), flip over, then lift off the top plate. Dust with icing sugar and serve warm.

limoncello sponge

ready in 1 hour 10 minutes, plus cooling | serves 8

This is a lovely light, lemony sponge flavoured with lemon liqueur and filled with strawberries. Most sponges are best eaten the day they are made, but this one keeps moist a little longer because of the addition of sour cream (that's if you can leave it alone!).

150g unsalted butter, cubed and
   softened
200g caster sugar
finely grated zest of 2 lemons
2 medium (size 6) free-range
   eggs and 1 extra yolk, at room
   temperature
125g standard flour
1 tsp baking powder
150g sour cream

lemon syrup
2½ Tbsp caster sugar
juice of 2 lemons

to finish
200ml cream
2 Tbsp limoncello liqueur
500g strawberries, hulled and
   sliced
icing sugar, for dusting

1 Preheat oven to 160°C (regular bake). Line the base of a 20cm cake tin with baking paper.

2 Put butter in a bowl and briefly beat with an electric beater until creamy and loose. Beat in caster sugar a tablespoon at a time, add lemon zest, and continue beating until fluffy and lighter in colour (creamed; see cooking class on page 111), stopping the machine and scraping down the sides of the bowl several times. Break eggs and extra yolk into a small bowl and beat with a fork until combined. Gradually beat eggs into the creamed butter and sugar, adding 2 tablespoons of the measured flour halfway through to help stabilise the mixture.

3 Sift remaining flour and the baking powder together onto a piece of paper, then sift this over the beaten egg mixture and fold in, along with the sour cream, using a large spoon.

4 Spoon mixture into prepared tin and smooth the top with a knife. Bake for about 40 minutes, or until the cake is golden brown on top and slightly shrinking from the sides of the tin, and springs back when lightly touched with the finger.

5 Cool in the tin for 10 minutes, then turn cake out onto a cooling rack and peel off paper. Leave to cool fully.

6 To make the syrup, stir sugar and lemon juice together until sugar dissolves. When cake is cool, return it to the tin, poke about 20 small holes through the cake with a fine skewer and pour over the syrup. Leave cake for at least 15 minutes.

7 Whip cream until it holds its shape, then stir in the limoncello. Cut sponge into two rounds with a large serrated knife and fill the middle with most of the limoncello cream and one-third of the strawberries. Spread remaining cream on top of sponge and arrange the rest of the strawberries on top. Dust generously with icing sugar and serve.

strawberry fairy cake

ready in 1 hour 30 minutes, plus cooling | serves 8

Fans of strawberries and cream will go into raptures over this light-as-a-feather cake. It's possibly at its best just after assembling, but I rather like it after it's spent a day reposing in the refrigerator, during which time the juice of the berries runs through the sponge and it all gets squishy and soft.

On the surface it looks easy enough to make, but care must be taken not to whip the whites too stiff (especially if using a large cake mixer) or they will become dry and difficult to blend with the other ingredients; and to add the flour in small lots, cutting and folding it in with a large spoon without decreasing the volume of the foam.

1 Preheat oven to 190°C (regular bake). Choose a tin with a diameter of 20cm, a depth of 6–7cm and, preferably, a removable base. Grease with a little melted butter, then line the sides and base with baking paper.

2 Sift flour, salt and 1 teaspoon of the cream of tartar onto a piece of paper. Whisk egg whites in a grease-free bowl until stiff, then sift over the other teaspoon of cream of tartar and 1 tablespoon of the caster sugar. Gradually whisk in the remaining sugar. The mixture should be stiff, but not dry and hard; when the uplifted beater is gently shaken, the whites should still have the merest wobble. Sprinkle vanilla extract and lemon juice over and mix in. Sift one-quarter of the flour mixture over the surface of the whipped egg whites and fold in carefully with a large spoon. Repeat with the rest of the flour mixture, adding in three lots, being careful not to knock out air (see cooking class on page 32).

3 Spoon mixture into the tin, level the surface with a knife, then bake for 20 minutes. Reduce heat to 170°C and bake for a further 15–20 minutes, or until the cake is a light golden brown, springy to the touch and pulling away from the sides of the tin. Remove cake from the oven and cool in the tin for 2–3 minutes only, then carefully invert onto a cooling rack lined with baking paper, and peel off paper from bottom of cake if attached.

4 One hour before finishing off the cake, put the strawberries in a bowl and sprinkle them with the icing sugar. Leave until the juices run, stirring once or twice.

5 When cake is cool, cut into two rounds with a serrated knife. Put the bottom half on a serving plate. Lightly whip the cream until it is just holding its shape but still falling off the whisk in dollops. Spread half the cream on the sponge bottom. Spoon over half the strawberries, then top with the other round of sponge. Cover the top with the rest of the cream and the rest of the strawberries. Serve immediately, or refrigerate until required.

75g standard flour
pinch of salt
2 tsp cream of tartar
6 medium (size 6) free-range egg whites, at room temperature
175g caster sugar
1 tsp vanilla extract
1 Tbsp lemon juice
350g fresh strawberries, hulled and sliced
3 Tbsp icing sugar
250ml cream

plum or nectarine friands

ready in 40 minutes | makes 12

Light, buttery and crisp-edged, these friands are just the thing for a little mid-afternoon tête-à-tête with copious pots of tea. Peaches or feijoas can also be used. Special friand tins are available, but I use non-stick Tupperware bakeware.

70g standard flour

240g icing sugar

150g ground almonds

finely grated zest of 1 lemon

6 medium (size 6) free-range egg
   whites, at room temperature

150g unsalted butter, melted

4 perfectly ripe nectarines, diced
   (should yield 1½ cups diced
   fruit), or 5–6 dark-fleshed plums,
   diced

icing sugar, for dusting

1 Preheat oven to 180°C (fanbake).

2 Sift flour and icing sugar together into a large bowl. Mix in ground almonds and lemon zest.

3 Lightly whisk egg whites until they form a firm snow (don't beat them as stiff as for a meringue, or they will be difficult to mix into the other ingredients). Add a little more than half the beaten egg whites to the dry ingredients and mix in with a large spoon. The mixture will be stiff and it will be a little difficult to mix in the egg whites; this is as it should be. Pour the melted butter around the sides of the batter – not over the top of it – then put the rest of the egg white on the top. Fold everything together gently, until just combined; don't beat. Carefully stir through nectarines (or plums).

4 Spoon mixture into 12 non-stick friand tins, filling them just a little more than three-quarters full. Bake for 15–20 minutes, or until risen and a pale golden colour.

5 Cool friands in the tins for 7–10 minutes, then turn them out onto a cooling rack. Dust with icing sugar before serving.

baby cakes with limoncello icing

ready in 50 minutes, plus cooling | makes 9–10

The craze for cupcakes may have abated, but when well made – light and buttery and topped with a sweet and creamy icing – they're pretty irresistible.

1 Preheat oven to 180°C (regular bake). Prepare paper cupcake cases inside a muffin tray.

2 Put butter in a bowl and beat with an electric beater until creamy and loose. Beat in caster sugar a tablespoon at a time and continue beating until fluffy and lighter in colour (creamed; see cooking class on page 111). You'll need to stop the machine and scrape down the sides of the bowl several times. Beat eggs together with a fork, then add them gradually to the creamed butter and sugar, adding 2–3 tablespoons of the measured flour halfway through beating to help stabilise the mixture. Stir in the vanilla extract.

3 Sift remaining flour and the baking powder together onto a piece of paper, then sift this over the creamed butter and eggs. Fold in with a large spoon, then mix in the milk.

4 Use two teaspoons to put the mixture into the paper cases by scooping the mixture up with one of the teaspoons, and using the other to scrape it into the paper case. Bake for 15 minutes, or until the cakes are an even, light golden brown and springy to the touch. Let them cool in the paper cases on a cooling rack.

5 To make the icing, put butter in a smallish bowl and whip until light and creamy. Beat in half the icing sugar in two or three lots, then stir in the limoncello. Beat in the remaining icing sugar. Swirl icing on top of cooled baby cakes and garnish each with a sliver of fresh lemon.

baby cakes
125g unsalted butter, cubed and softened
115g caster sugar
2 medium (size 6) free-range eggs, at room temperature
120g standard flour
½ tsp vanilla extract
2 tsp baking powder
60ml milk, at room temperature

limoncello icing
110g unsalted butter, softened
175g icing sugar, sifted
1 Tbsp limoncello liqueur
a few slices fresh lemon cut into small wedges (optional)

little nectarine sponge cakes

ready in 40 minutes, plus cooling | makes 12

These are gorgeously light to eat and will fit any occasion – from brunch, morning or afternoon tea, to dessert, teamed with homemade custard. The batter can also be made into one large cake – spoon it into a 23cm cake tin lined on the base and sides with baking paper and bake for 30–35 minutes.

200g standard flour

3 tsp baking powder

6 firmish but ripe nectarines

spiced sugar (mix 2 Tbsp caster
   sugar, 1 tsp ground cinnamon
   and ½ tsp mixed spice), for
   sprinkling

2 medium (size 6) free-range eggs,
   at room temperature

225g caster sugar

125g unsalted butter

170ml milk

icing sugar, for dusting (optional)

1 Preheat oven to 200°C (regular bake). Have deep paper cases (½ cup capacity) ready on a baking sheet.

2 Sift flour and baking powder together onto a piece of paper. Set aside. Slice nectarines. Mix up the spiced sugar in a small bowl.

3 Break eggs into a bowl and whisk with an electric beater for 1 minute, then whisk in the 225g measure of caster sugar a tablespoonful at a time (see cooking class on page 32). Continue whisking until the mixture is pale, thick and mousse-like, and will form a ribbon when the beaters are lifted out of the mixture (the mixture should fall off the beaters in a thick trail).

4 Meanwhile, put butter and milk in a saucepan and heat gently until butter has melted. Sift half the flour and baking powder mixture over the egg mousse and fold in with a large spoon, then sift the rest over and fold in. Bring the butter and milk to a quick boil and pour, still bubbling, into the cake batter, stirring continuously. Mix until smooth (don't worry about small lumps as they will cook out).

5 Spoon batter into each paper case to two-thirds full. Arrange sliced nectarines on top, putting in enough so that the batter and fruit come to just below the top of the paper case. Sprinkle with spiced sugar. Bake for 25–30 minutes, until golden on top. The cakes will feel very soft but should not be wobbly. If liked, dust with icing sugar.

feijoa cake with crumble topping

ready in 1 hour, plus cooling | serves 8

Our favourite Kiwi backyard fruit tree, the feijoa, may hail from Brazil, but we have made it our own. It's the intoxicating perfume – a mix of pineapple, banana, guava, melon and pear – that turns heads, and the lemony tang and lingering, ripe strawberry–banana taste that wins people over. The creamy-coloured flesh is granular like a pear in some varieties and smooth in others, but when perfectly ripe all have clear jellied sections in the centre. Feijoas make an excellent crumble combined with banana, as in this recipe, or to add interest to apple crumble.

crumble topping
70g standard white flour
80g light brown sugar, sifted
¾ tsp mixed spice
50g unsalted butter, melted
50g slivered almonds

cake
75g unsalted butter
finely grated zest of 2 lemons and 1 Tbsp lemon juice
1 ripe banana
4 large feijoas, mashed
140g standard flour
pinch of salt
1 level tsp baking powder
4 medium (size 6) free-range eggs, at room temperature
165g caster sugar
icing sugar, for dusting

1 Preheat oven to 180°C (regular bake). Line base and sides of a 23cm cake tin with baking paper.

2 To make crumble topping, blend flour, sugar and mixed spice in a bowl, squishing any lumps. Pour over melted butter, mix in with a fork, then stir in almonds. Set aside.

3 To make the cake, melt butter gently, then leave to cool. Grate zest from lemons and set aside. Peel and mash banana. Halve feijoas, scoop out flesh and mash. Mix mashed fruit with lemon juice. Sift flour with salt and baking powder onto a piece of paper.

4 Break eggs into a bowl and whisk with an electric beater for 1 minute, then whisk in the caster sugar a tablespoon at a time (see cooking class on page 32). Continue whisking until the mixture is pale, thick and mousse-like, and will form a ribbon when the beaters are lifted above the mixture (the mixture should fall off the beaters in a thick trail; see cooking class on page 32). Sprinkle the lemon zest over.

5 Sift half the dry ingredients over the egg mixture and fold in lightly with a large spoon. Pour the cooled butter around the sides of the bowl. Fold together gently until just combined. Sieve and fold in the rest of the dry ingredients, then fold in the fruit.

6 Pour into prepared tin. Gently scatter the crumble topping over, taking care not to deflate the cake batter. Bake for 30–40 minutes or until cake is springy to the touch, golden and pulling away from the sides of the tin. Remove from oven and let it rest for 15 minutes. Invert onto a plate, peel off paper if still attached, cover with a cooling rack and turn it right side up again. Leave to cool completely. Dust with icing sugar before serving.

sugar-crust sponge with passionfruit icing

ready in 50 minutes, plus cooling | serves 8

This classic sponge recipe never lets me down. Fill it with seasonal fruit and cream, whipped cream mixed with lemon curd, or bananas and cream. Top with drippy passionfruit icing.

1 Preheat oven to 170°C (regular bake). Prepare a 21cm cake tin by brushing lightly with butter. Put a disc of baking paper on the base of the tin and brush this with butter as well. Put a heaped tablespoon of caster sugar in the tin and shake it around to coat the bottom and sides. Tap out the excess. Repeat with a tablespoon of flour, tapping out excess.

2 Sift flour and salt together onto a piece of paper to aerate. In a bowl, whisk eggs with an electric beater until frothy, then whisk in caster sugar a tablespoon at a time and keep whisking until mixture is pale, thick and mousse-like, and will form a ribbon when the beaters are lifted out of the mixture (the mixture should fall off the beater in a thick trail; see cooking class on page 32).

3 Sift flour mixture over the top of the whisked eggs and sugar, then carefully fold it in using a large spoon or rubber spatula, adding the lemon zest. Take care not to knock out the air (see cooking class on page 32).

4 Bake for 15–20 minutes or until light golden in colour, springy to the touch and just starting to pull away from the sides of the tin (this may take as long as 25 minutes, but do not let it get too brown or it can become dry). Cool for 2–3 minutes in the tin, then turn out onto a piece of baking paper set over a cooling rack, and peel off the paper from the bottom of the sponge. Leave to cool completely before assembling with the cream.

5 Peel banana and slice thinly, then squeeze the lemon juice over and stir gently to coat the slices. Whip cream until firmish and holding its shape. Cut sponge into two rounds with a large serrated knife (a bread knife is good; use gentle sawing movements). Spread bottom half of sponge with cream and arrange banana on top. Put top half of sponge in place.

6 Mix icing sugar with passionfruit pulp. The icing should just fall off the spoon. If it is too thick, add a few drops of water. If it is too thin, simply add more icing sugar. Carefully brush off any crumbs from top of cake, then pour on icing. Spread with a flat-bladed knife, taking it to the edge of the sponge and encouraging it to drip down. Cut into portions once the icing has set.

sponge
110g standard flour
pinch of salt
3 medium (size 6) free-range eggs,
    at room temperature
125g caster sugar
finely grated zest of 1 lemon
1 large banana
juice of ½ lemon
150ml cream

passionfruit icing
120–160g icing sugar, sifted
pulp from 1–2 passionfruit

A cooking class with Julie

Making cakes

For baking, it's important that ingredients are measured accurately. It is better to weigh dry ingredients rather than use cup measures, because a lightly filled cup will not weigh as much as a heavily filled one. If you don't have scales, check the guide on page 172 (weights and measures). Spoon measures are level. Liquids are measured in jugs viewed at eye level, not from above.

Eggs are essential for the lightness of cakes, as on heating they expand and coagulate and so hold any air beaten into the mixture. Buy them fresh and use at room temperature. Use unsalted butter. Use the flour specified in the recipe. Replace spices often, ensuring they are fresh.

Many modern ovens have a fanbake option. This is a hotter, drier way of cooking which suits some foods, but not all. Use it to roast meats and vegetables and to cook some pastry dishes, but not for cakes, custards and other dishes where gentle heat is recommended. If your oven doesn't have a fanbake option, and the recipe calls for fanbaking, increase the given temperature by 10°C.

Sponge cakes made with whole eggs and no added butter are best eaten the day of baking, as they soon dry out. They are superb split and filled with fresh fruit and whipped cream. When cutting a soft cake such as a sponge, use a large, sharp, serrated bread knife with gentle sawing movements to avoid squashing the cake crumb. Once cut, cakes can be moved around easily and safely using a cake slide (picture 1). Cakes with added butter will keep fresh and moist for 3–4 days.

Traditional English cake-making methods fall into four groups:

- **Whisking method**
  Eggs and sugar are whisked over a gentle heat, or with an electric cake mixer, until a thick, stable foam forms; then flour is folded in with a large spoon. In some recipes, the eggs are first separated and the whipped whites are added along with the flour. In a third method, melted butter is poured into the bowl around the sides of the cake mixture and carefully and quickly folded in. (See page 32.)

- **Rubbing-in method**
  Cubed butter is rubbed through flour by picking it up with the fingers and letting it slip through fingers and thumbs while gently pressing it together, until the mixture resembles coarse breadcrumbs; then a small amount of liquid is added to bind (see page 82).

- **Creaming method**
  Butter and sugar are beaten together until fluffy and pale in colour (this is called 'creamed'), then lightly beaten eggs are added gradually, and then the dry ingredients and any other liquids (see page 111).

- **Warming or melting method**
  The fat, usually butter, is warmed with sugar or syrup, and sometimes also with the liquid (or part of it) that is called for in the recipe, until the butter melts and the sugar dissolves or the syrup liquefies. The melted mixture is then cooled before stirring into the dry ingredients. (See page 165.)

1

Tin preparation

Before commencing baking, prepare any tins which are called for because with most methods there should be no delay between mixing and baking. The best cake tins are the oldest – so grab your mother's or grandmother's! Failing that, aluminium pans will give the best result, as aluminium is heat-absorbing and conducts heat evenly. Shiny tins should be avoided as they reflect heat (aluminium is dull). New black metal tins absorb heat but can cause over-browning; older darkened well-worn-in aluminium tins are ideal.

Avoid washing cake tins if you can (never put them in the dishwasher); instead, wipe them out with paper towels while still warm. They will eventually build up a baked-on coating which prevents sticking. If they are old and prone to rust, rub with a little oil.

Melted lard is ideal for brushing over cake tins as it glides on smoothly and leaves a thin film, but it is not a popular choice these days. You are most likely to use vegetable sprays, which with careful application give an even coating, or butter. If using butter, make sure it is unsalted (salted butter can cause sticking); brush it on while it is melted, then rub gently with a paper towel to remove excess. The whole tin should be greased, and the bottom of the tin lined with paper if called for in the recipe, and the paper greased, too. The tin is then dusted with flour and the excess tapped out. If the cake tin is only greased and not floured, the cake will slip as it rises; dusting the tin with flour helps it grip the tin.

Lining a tin

Lining a cake tin makes it easier to turn the cake out, and it also offers some protection to the sides and bottom of the cake as it cooks. Baking paper is ideal for lining cake tins because it is non-stick.

To line the base of a cake tin, use a pencil to trace around the base of the tin on baking paper and cut slightly inside the pencil mark.

To line the sides, cut a wide band of paper long enough to go around the sides of the tin; this band should be marginally higher than the tin, so that once it is folded it is roughly the same height as the tin. Fold over one edge of the paper, then snip it with scissors about every centimetre or so (picture 1). This helps it fit around the inside of the cake tin. Put the band of paper in the tin, with the snipped edge towards the bottom, then put the round of paper on top of the snipped edge (pictures 2 and 3).

Spoon the cake mixture into the tin, putting it in the centre of the tin first and spreading it to the sides without disturbing the paper lining.

If a crisp crust is desired on a whisked sponge, the tins are first greased and the bottom lined with paper and that is also greased, then everything is sprinkled with caster sugar (picture 4). The sugar is shaken around the tin until the sides and bottom are coated, then the tin is turned upside down and given a tap to release excess sugar. Next it is dusted with flour, the excess tapped out as described for sugar. The sugar makes it crisp; the flour merely fills in any holes. The tin for a chocolate sponge is not prepared with sugar, as this would make the outside of the sponge too sweet. Chocolate often forms a crust of its own.

Preheating the oven and setting racks in position

Before starting food preparation, preheat the oven, getting the racks in the right position. Most cakes should be cooked in the centre of the oven where there is good circulation of air. This means the rack should be set below the centre of the oven, so that when the cake is put on the rack, the top and middle of it will be roughly in the middle of the oven. If the rack is put in the centre of the oven, the top of the cake will be in the top-third of the oven and it can become over-brown and dry out. Heavy fruit cakes are generally cooked lower down in the oven.

Using the whisking method

Whisked sponges are the lightest of all the English cakes, containing only a small proportion of flour. They are often called 'fatless sponges' as they do not contain fat, apart from that which is in the egg yolks. They are entirely dependent on the amount of air beaten in with the eggs. Eggs are best about 3–5 days old and give more volume when used at room temperature.

The basic method is to whisk eggs and sugar in a bowl over a gentle heat until thick and mousse-like – resting the bowl over a small saucepan of very hot water does the trick – so that the mixture will form a thick trail when the whisk is lifted out of the mixture (picture 1). The heat helps increase the volume of the eggs and sugar. It's not necessary if using an electric cake mixer, which forms a thick, stable foam and warms the mixture through agitation, but excellent results can be gained by whisking eggs and sugar over a gentle heat using a hand-held electric beater. It's important that the bottom of the bowl doesn't touch the water – you're not after cooked eggs!

1

Start by beating the eggs on a low speed, then increase the speed as they thicken. Add sugar gradually, scraping down the sides of the bowl from time to time to ensure all the sugar is mixed in. If sugar crystals are left undissolved on the side of the bowl, they will form speckles on top of the cake. Use caster sugar, as granulated sugar is too coarse and does not dissolve as readily. It will take about 10 minutes to achieve a thick and stable foam using a hand-held electric beater; longer if using a hand whisk and elbow grease. Once the mixture is thick enough, remove bowl from heat and continue beating for 3–4 minutes, until it cools.

Flour settles as it stands in a bag or container, becoming heavy, and needs to be well sifted to aerate it before using in cake making. Use fine flour and sift it three times, adding a pinch of salt for flavour and any dry flavourings called for in the recipe (picture 2). Sift it over the top of the whisked eggs and sugar (picture 3), without banging the sieve on the bowl, then carefully fold in using a large spoon or rubber spatula. Care

2

3

4

5

6

7

must be taken not to knock out the air. The best method is to run the spoon around the side of the bowl, then turn the spoon over and let the scooped mixture fall back on itself in the centre of the bowl (pictures 4 to 6). Next, use the spoon to cut through the middle of the mixture, scooping down to the bottom of the bowl, and let the mixture fall off the spoon on to itself again. Give the bowl a quarter turn and repeat 'cutting and folding' the mixture together until no pockets of unmixed flour remain. Turn the mixture into the prepared tin (picture 7) and gently tilt to even the top if necessary, or spread level with a knife, as it will not find its own level during baking. Do not bang or drop the cake tin because it will knock out air.

In some recipes, the eggs are first separated, the yolks are creamed with sugar and the stiffly whipped egg whites are added along with the flour. In a third method, melted butter is poured in around the sides of the cake mixture, rather than over the top, which can deflate the mixture, and is carefully and quickly folded in. The butter must be heated just to melting and shouldn't be too hot, and mixing should be carried out until everything is just combined. Complete mixing while pouring batter into the tin, ensuring there is no unmixed batter on the bottom of the bowl.

Whisked mixtures are delicate, and there should be no delays between mixing and baking – bake immediately. The standard oven temperature for a whisked sponge is 180°C. Avoid opening the oven door until three-quarters of the specified time has passed, as the mixture easily sinks if cooled by air before it is set in position. If cooking two sponges on different levels, you will have to swap their positions during baking, but not until the cakes are set in position; and then, only open the door as much as needed. Ensure the kitchen is draught-free before doing so, as sudden changes in temperature can cause a sponge to sink.

A sponge cake is ready when it is golden brown on top and shrinking slightly from the sides of the tin. It should feel springy to the touch. Do not test with a skewer, because if tested too early this will deflate the cake.

Turn the cake out of the tin after 5–10 minutes to stop further cooking or sweating, which can cause shrinkage. Shake cake gently before turning it out, to make sure it is loose from the tin. If not, run a thin-bladed knife between sponge and tin to help loosen it. To turn out, put a light plate on top of the sponge, flip, remove tin and peel off paper if attached (it often remains in the tin) (picture 8). Now put a cooling rack on top, lined with baking paper to prevent the sponge sticking to the rack, flip, and lift off the plate. Allow the cake to cool away from draughts to ensure it cools evenly.

8

tarts and pies

crostata

ready in 1 hour, plus chilling and cooling | serves 8 or more

This is gorgeous to eat – the bee's knees of jam tarts – but you must use a good-quality jam in the filling. The milk keeps the pastry crust nice and tender. It's quickly made in a food processor.

1 Preheat oven to 180°C (fanbake). Have ready a 24cm loose-bottomed flan ring set on a baking sheet lined with baking paper.

2 To make the pastry, sift flour, salt, baking powder and sugar together, then transfer to the bowl of a food processor fitted with the chopping blade. Add butter and process until mixture resembles coarse breadcrumbs. Mix egg yolks and milk together and pour into the processor through the feed tube. Pulse just until mixture gathers in large clumps. Turn dough onto a dry, lightly floured surface and knead until smooth. Wrap in plastic food wrap and refrigerate for 15 minutes, just until firm.

3 Roll out pastry on a lightly floured surface and line into flan ring. Refrigerate for 15 minutes to firm pastry. Re-roll pastry scraps and cut into long strips. Chill until firm.

4 Mix lemon zest and jam, then spread over pastry in flan ring. Lay pastry strips in a criss-cross pattern on top. Have a baking sheet heating on a shelf in the centre of the oven. Slide flan and paper off cold baking sheet onto hot one in oven. Bake for 30 minutes, or until pastry is golden. Remove from oven, dust with icing sugar, then leave until cool enough to handle. Carefully remove from flan ring. Serve at room temperature.

300g standard flour
pinch of salt
1 tsp baking powder
100g caster sugar
150g unsalted butter, firm but pliable, cubed
2 medium (size 6) free-range egg yolks
60ml milk
finely grated zest of 1 lemon
370g jar black cherry or damson plum jam, or jam or conserve of your choice
icing sugar, for dusting

tart au citron

ready in: curd 20 minutes, plus cooling; tart 1 hour 20 minutes, plus chilling | serves 8 or more

This is a sophisticated dessert which may be a tad tricky for a beginner, but it's rewarding if you can pull it off. Allow plenty of time to make it, and make the pastry when the kitchen is cool. The lemon curd can be made several days in advance and the pastry can be made a day before serving – line it into the flan ring, cover and keep chilled, then assemble and bake the tart on the day. It can be cooked in the morning for dinner without any sign of deterioration. It will keep well for 2–3 days.

lemon curd
120g unsalted butter
200g caster sugar
zest and juice of 2 large lemons
3 large (size 7) free-range eggs

almond pastry
180g standard flour
pinch of salt
100g ground almonds
180g unsalted butter
120g caster sugar
1 egg and 2 egg yolks, all medium (size 6) free-range eggs
2 drops vanilla extract

to finish
1 free-range egg white, lightly beaten, to glaze
caster sugar, for dusting

1 To make the lemon curd, put the butter in a china or heatproof-glass mixing bowl and set it over a pan of simmering water. Heat gently until melted, then add remaining ingredients. Stir over a low to medium heat until thick – when it coats the spoon thickly. The curd will take about 15 minutes to thicken; don't hurry it along or it may curdle – the eggs will scramble! Remove from the heat, and cool.

2 To make the pastry, sift flour and salt onto a pastry board or a smooth, dry surface. Make a well in the centre, pushing the flour out to the side, and sprinkle the ground almonds over the flour. Put butter between two pieces of greaseproof paper and press flat into a cake with a rolling pin. Put the butter in the centre of the ring of flour, then sprinkle sugar over the butter. Use one of the eggs to make hollows in the sugar, then break the egg and nestle it with and the egg yolks into these hollows. Sprinkle vanilla over. Work butter, sugar, eggs and vanilla together with the fingertips of one hand, pecking at them like a chicken pecks at grain. Use only your fingertips to keep things cool; the hand gets warmer towards the palm. When thoroughly blended, draw in the flour and almonds (a plastic pastry scraper is useful). Rinse and dry your mixing hand (to stop dry flakes on your hand getting into the pastry), then knead pastry gently into a ball, dusting with a little flour to stop sticking. Wrap in plastic food wrap and chill until firm – up to 1 hour only or it will be difficult to roll.

3 Cut off one-third of the pastry and set aside for the top of the tart. Roll out the rest into a round and line into a 23cm flan ring set on a baking sheet lined with baking paper. Prick pastry with a fork. Roll the pastry for the top into a round, making sure it is big enough to cover the top of the flan. Chill only until firm.

4 Preheat oven to 180°C (regular bake). Fill the flan base three-quarters full with lemon curd. Put top pastry in place and seal edges together.

5 Bake for 40 minutes, draping tart with tin foil after the first 20–30 minutes to prevent crust over-browning. Remove tart from oven, lift off foil, then brush with lightly beaten egg white and dust with caster sugar. Return to oven for 8–10 minutes to frost the top. Serve cold.

rhubarb and almond tart

ready in 1 hour 5 minutes, plus chilling and cooling | serves 8

If you grow rhubarb, twist – don't cut – the stalks off the plant, as they will keep longer; and remove leaves immediately (the leaves contain oxalic acid, which is poisonous and potentially life-threatening). The stalks are perfectly safe to eat, though they still contain enough oxalic acid to hinder absorption of the plant's plentiful supply of calcium and iron. Rhubarb is still a worthwhile food as it contains a good amount of fibre, potassium and vitamin C. Ready-made sweet pastry generally browns more quickly than homemade rich shortcrust, so bake it blind just until it is colouring around the top rim.

500g rhubarb
75g caster sugar
400g ready-made sweet shortcrust
    or buttercrust pastry

topping
100g standard flour
100g light muscovado sugar
1 tsp mixed spice
75g unsalted butter, melted
70g slivered almonds
icing sugar, for dusting

1 Preheat oven to 180°C (fanbake). Set a 23cm loose-bottomed flan ring on a baking sheet lined with baking paper.

2 Wash and trim rhubarb and cut into short lengths. Put rhubarb in a shallow baking dish and sprinkle with caster sugar. Cover with tin foil and bake for 15–20 minutes, or until just tender (after 15 minutes' cooking time, check rhubarb every minute because it quickly blows open and turns to mush). Transfer to a large sieve to drain (reserve juices; they are delicious served with cereal or ice cream).

3 Roll out pastry on a lightly floured surface and line into flan ring. Prick pastry base with a fork, then refrigerate until firm. To bake blind, line pastry with light tin foil or crumpled tissue paper and fill with baking beans (see cooking class on page 83). Bake for 15 minutes, or until pastry is set in place and has coloured around the rim.

4 Remove the pastry case from the oven and lift off the tin foil or paper and baking beans. Return the pastry case to the oven for a further 3–5 minutes, until the inside of the pastry is dry and no longer buttery. Remove from oven. Increase oven temperature to 190°C (fanbake).

5 To make the topping, put flour, muscovado sugar and mixed spice in a mixing bowl and blend with a spoon, squishing any lumps. Pour on melted butter, mix in with a fork, then stir in slivered almonds.

6 To assemble, arrange rhubarb in pastry case and spoon almond topping over. Bake for 20 minutes, or until golden on top. Cool for 10–15 minutes in the flan ring, then remove flan ring and base and rest tart on a cooling rack. Serve warm, dusted with icing sugar.

apple tartlets

ready in 55 minutes, plus chilling | makes 8

A single tartlet makes an elegant dessert. If serving these for a dinner party, you could make the pastry and line it into the tins ahead of time, then freeze pastry in the tins. Once frozen, flip pastry bases out and transfer to a sealable plastic bag. On the day, return them to their tins, thaw them in the refrigerator and carry on with the recipe.

sweet rich shortcrust pastry
225g standard flour
pinch of salt
1 Tbsp caster sugar
170g unsalted butter, firm but
    pliable
1 medium (size 6) free-range
    egg yolk
4–5 Tbsp chilled water

apple topping
3 large (size 7) free-range
    egg yolks
200ml cream
75g caster sugar
800g (about 4 large) Granny Smith
    or cooking apples

apricot glaze
1 small jar inexpensive apricot jam
1 Tbsp lemon juice

1 To make the pastry, sift flour, salt and sugar together, then transfer to the bowl of a food processor fitted with the chopping blade. Add butter and process briefly until the mixture resembles coarse breadcrumbs. Mix egg yolk and 4 tablespoons water together and pour into the processor through the feed tube. Pulse until mixture gathers in large clumps. If you don't have a food processor, put flour, sugar and salt in a large mixing bowl and cut the butter through the flour using two knives or a pastry blender, then rub in with the fingers until it resembles coarse crumbs (see cooking class on page 58). Add the egg yolk mixed with 5 tablespoons of water and mix to a dough. Tip dough onto a dry, lightly floured surface and knead until smooth. Wrap in plastic food wrap and refrigerate for 30 minutes.

2 Roll out pastry thinly on a lightly floured surface and line into eight loose-bottomed 10cm diameter metal tartlet tins (if necessary, re-roll scraps and cut out more rounds). Prick bottom of tartlets with a fork and chill until pastry is firm.

3 Preheat oven to 180°C (fanbake). Put tartlets on a baking sheet and line each with a double thickness of tissue paper or thin tin foil (see cooking class on page 83). Fill with baking beans and bake for about 15 minutes, or until the pastry is set in shape and has coloured around the rim. Remove paper or foil and baking beans.

4 To make the topping, put egg yolks in a large bowl and beat with a small hand whisk. Beat in the cream and 3 tablespoons of the sugar to form a custard. Peel the apples, cut in half and remove the cores. Slice thinly. Arrange apples in the pastry cases, neatly if liked, then pour the custard over. Sprinkle with the rest of the sugar.

5 Bake the tartlets in the top third of the oven for about 25 minutes, or until the pastry is golden and the apples are browned and lightly charred in some places. Remove from the oven and cool for 10 minutes.

6 Slip the tartlets out of the tins and put them on a cooling rack. Make the apricot glaze as on page 154 and brush the apples and pastry rim with hot glaze. Leave tartlets to cool completely before serving.

rough and tumble peach tart

ready in 1 hour 10 minutes, plus chilling | serves 8

The pastry for this free-form tart is quickly made in a food processor. It calls for perfect sweet peaches that are slightly firm, not early-season fruit which is often sour or bitter. Look for free-stone peaches, a term which denotes that the peaches will readily break apart and the stones can be removed easily. Cling-stone implies that the fruit sticks to the stones. Cling-stone peaches can still be used for this recipe – use a small, sharp knife to cut fruit into wedges by cutting into the stone and releasing the peach slices. For a change, use apricots or plums in place of peaches.

1 To make the pastry, sift flour, salt, cinnamon and sugar together, then transfer to the bowl of a food processor fitted with the chopping blade. Add butter and process briefly until the mixture resembles coarse breadcrumbs. Add water through the feed tube and pulse until mixture gathers in large clumps. Tip dough onto a dry, lightly floured surface and knead until smooth. Wrap in plastic food wrap and refrigerate for 30 minutes, or until firm.

2 Preheat oven to 180°C (fanbake). Roll out pastry to a 30cm round on a lightly floured surface. Transfer to a baking sheet lined with baking paper.

3 To make the filling, peel and stone the peaches and cut flesh into wedges. Toss peaches with lemon juice in a bowl and leave them to macerate (soften and soak up flavour) for 5 minutes. Mix in the first measure of caster sugar, the lemon zest and flour, and pile fruit into the centre of the pastry. Fold in pastry edges by about 4cm, pinching the dough together to make it stay in place.

4 Scatter a few almonds on top of the peaches. Mix remaining almonds with the beaten egg white and paste them onto the outside of the pastry edging. Dust pastry with the second measure of caster sugar. Bake tart for 35–40 minutes, or until the pastry is golden and the fruit tender. Dust with icing sugar before serving.

pastry

300g standard flour

pinch of salt

¼ tsp ground cinnamon

2 Tbsp caster sugar

150g unsalted butter, firm but pliable

100ml chilled water

filling

8 perfectly ripe peaches

2 Tbsp lemon juice

2 Tbsp caster sugar

finely grated zest of 1 lemon

3 Tbsp standard flour

70g slivered almonds

1 medium (size 6) free-range egg white, lightly beaten

2 Tbsp caster sugar

icing sugar, for dusting

apricot and almond tart

ready in 1 hour 10 minutes, plus chilling | serves at least 8

Serve this as an afternoon tea treat – with copious cups of tea and a plate of homemade biscuits you can stretch it to around 12 servings – or for dessert with a bowl of whipped cream or thick yoghurt.

sweet rich shortcrust pastry

225g standard flour
pinch of salt
1 Tbsp caster sugar
170g unsalted butter, firm but pliable
1 medium (size 6) free-range egg yolk
5 Tbsp chilled water

filling

125g unsalted butter, softened
170g caster sugar, plus extra for sprinkling
2 medium (size 6) free-range eggs, plus 1 extra yolk, at room temperature
4 Tbsp standard flour
140g ground almonds
160g apricot jam
12 apricots (or plums)

to finish

icing sugar, for dusting

1 Preheat oven to 180°C (fanbake). Have ready a rectangular loose-bottomed cake tin, 28cm × 24cm, or a 22cm flan ring, set on a baking sheet.

2 To make the pastry, sift flour and salt into a large bowl. Stir caster sugar through. Drop in butter and cut in with two knives or a pastry blender (see cooking class on page 82). Beat egg yolk with chilled water. Mix dry ingredients and butter to a stiff dough with egg yolk and water, adding a little extra water if the dough is flaky and dry. Knead dough gently and wrap in plastic food wrap. Refrigerate for 20 minutes to firm. Alternatively, make pastry in a food processor as described in recipe for apple tartlets (page 40).

3 Roll out pastry on a lightly floured surface and line into tin. Refrigerate again for 15 minutes to firm.

4 To make the filling, put butter in a bowl and beat briefly until creamy and loose. Beat in caster sugar a tablespoon at a time and continue beating until fluffy and lighter in colour (creamed; see cooking class on page 111). You'll need to stop the machine and scrape the sides of the bowl down several times. Break eggs into a bowl, add extra yolk, and beat lightly with a fork. Sprinkle flour over creamed butter and sugar, then with machine running gradually beat in eggs. Fold in almonds with a large spoon.

5 Prick chilled pastry with a fork, then line with tin foil and fill with baking beans (see cooking class on page 83). Bake blind for 15 minutes, until pastry is set in place and has coloured around the rim. Remove from oven and take out tin foil and baking beans. Spread the pastry base with apricot jam.

6 Halve fruit and remove stones. Spread almond filling over pastry, then arrange fruit cut side up. Sprinkle with caster sugar.

7 Bake the tart in the lower third of the oven for 25 minutes, then drape a piece of tin foil over the top of the tart to protect it, and bake for another 10 minutes until filling is nearly set – it will still have a little wobble in the centre. Cool before serving. Dust with icing sugar and serve.

lime and coconut tartlets

ready in 40 minutes, plus chilling and cooling | makes 24

Crispy coconut meringue over tangy lime curd makes for a taste explosion. For a change, try these tartlets with lemon or passionfruit curd, and use the coconut meringue to top other tarts. If using the tartlet tray to make a second batch of tarts, wash, dry and grease it and make sure it is cool before assembling.

4 pre-rolled frozen sheets sweet shortcrust pastry, about 24cm × 24cm each, thawed just before using
2 medium (size 6) free-range egg whites, at room temperature
120g caster sugar
60g desiccated coconut
370g jar ready-made lime curd

1 Preheat oven to 175°C (fanbake). Lightly grease a shallow 24-hole tartlet tray with holes 6cm wide by 3cm deep, or bake two batches in a 12-hole tray.

2 Cut out 24 rounds of pastry with a 7.5cm pastry cutter. Line into tartlet tray and chill until firm.

3 Beat egg whites with a hand-held electric beater until stiff. Add sugar gradually, and continue beating until stiff and glossy. Fold in coconut. Spoon lime curd into pastry rounds in tray.

4 Spread coconut topping evenly over lime curd layer, making sure the curd is completely covered. Bake tartlets for about 15 minutes, or until pastry rims are golden and coconut meringue is browned. Cool tarts in the tray for 5 minutes, or until pastry is firm, then gently loosen them from the tray with a knife and turn them out onto a cooling rack. Serve at room temperature.

bakewell tart

ready in 1 hour, plus chilling and cooling | serves 8

This English tart has its origins in the 15th century. It was essentially a jam custard pudding, which in modern times was thickened with ground almonds and cooked in a pastry case. Lemon and desiccated coconut are good improvements.

1 Preheat oven to 180°C (fanbake). Have ready a 22cm loose-bottom flan ring set on a baking sheet lined with baking paper.

2 To make the pastry, sift flour with salt to aerate. Put butter and flour in the bowl of a food processor fitted with the chopping blade. Process briefly until the mixture resembles coarse breadcrumbs. Mix egg yolk and 4 tablespoons water together and pour into the processor through the feed tube. Pulse just until dough gathers in clumps. If you don't have a food processor, put flour and salt in a large mixing bowl and cut the butter through the flour using two knives or a pastry blender, then rub in with the fingers until it resembles coarse crumbs (see cooking class on page 58). Add the egg yolk mixed with 5 tablespoons of water and mix to a dough. Tip dough onto a dry, lightly floured surface and knead until smooth. Wrap in plastic food wrap and refrigerate for 15 minutes until just firm.

3 Roll out dough on a lightly floured surface and line into flan ring. Refrigerate until pastry is firm.

4 To make the topping, use a hand-held electric beater to whip the butter until soft, then beat in sugar a tablespoon at a time, add lemon zest and beat until fluffy and lighter in colour. Beat eggs together in a small bowl and add them gradually to butter and sugar mixture. Stir in ground almonds, coconut and lemon juice.

5 Spread jam and lemon curd on pastry base, then spread topping over curd.

6 Have a baking sheet heating on the centre shelf in the oven. Slide flan and paper off cold baking sheet onto hot one in oven. Bake for 25–30 minutes, or until pastry is golden around the edges. Drape tart loosely with a piece of tin foil and cook for a further 15 minutes, or until pastry is cooked. Cool for 10 minutes on a cooling rack then remove flan ring, leaving tart on the metal base until further cooled. Carefully remove from metal base. Serve warmish or at room temperature.

rich shortcrust pastry
225g standard flour
pinch of salt
170g butter, firm but pliable
1 medium (size 6) free-range egg yolk
4–5 Tbsp chilled water

topping
60g unsalted butter, softened
100g caster sugar
grated and chopped zest and juice of 1 lemon
2 medium (size 6) free-range eggs, at room temperature
100g ground almonds
4 Tbsp desiccated coconut
2 Tbsp strawberry jam
2 Tbsp homemade (see page 36) or ready-made lemon curd

ali baba tartlets

ready in 40 minutes | makes 24

These tartlets can be kept at room temperature for 2–3 hours, but are best kept refrigerated if you are making them several hours ahead – bring to room temperature before serving. If you prefer a more uniform look, put the yoghurt in a piping bag fitted with a smallish plain nozzle and pipe it on top of the tartlets. It's important to use soft, supple dates – these will be miserable with old dried dates found in the back of the pantry.

2 pre-rolled frozen sheets sweet shortcrust pastry, about 24xcm × 24cm each, thawed just before using

250g fresh dates

50g flaked (sliced) almonds, for the top

50g unsalted butter, softened

finely grated zest of 1 lemon, and 1–2 Tbsp lemon juice

1 level Tbsp manuka or scented floral honey

250ml, or more, Greek-style yoghurt

1 Preheat oven to 180°C (fanbake).

2 Cut pastry sheets into 6cm rounds and line into a 24-hole tartlet tray (or bake two batches in a 12-hole tin). Line with thin tin foil, pushing the foil down onto the pastry, and fill with baking beans (see cooking class on page 83). Bake tartlet bases for 10–12 minutes, then carefully lift off foil and baking beans. If the pastry isn't nice and golden, return tartlet bases uncovered to the oven for 1–2 minutes to dry out and brown. Cool in the tin for 5 minutes, then flip them out with the point of a knife and leave to cool completely on a cooling rack.

3 Halve the dates, then pick out and discard stones. Slice flesh into thin strips. Put almonds in a shallow ovenproof dish and toast in an oven preheated to 180°C for 7–10 minutes, or until lightly browned. Transfer to a plate.

4 Put butter in a bowl and whip until soft and creamy. Add lemon zest and 1 tablespoon of juice, the honey and dates, and mix until smooth. Sharpen with more lemon juice if necessary. When tartlet bases are cold, fill with date mixture. Beat yoghurt until smooth, then spoon or pipe on top of dates. Top with a sprinkling of almonds and serve.

mum's apple and rhubarb pie

ready in 1 hour 20 minutes, plus chilling | serves 6–8

Enamel plates take me back to my childhood – my mother had them in various sizes, and I've found myself collecting them too. She made great pastry, and this is a tribute to her. The sweet smell as the pie cooks is tantalising and will have everyone popping into the kitchen asking when it will be ready to eat. Patience!

sweet rich shortcrust pastry
225g standard plain flour
pinch of salt
1 Tbsp caster sugar
170g butter, firm but pliable, cubed
1 medium (size 6) free-range egg yolk
4–5 Tbsp chilled water
a little milk and caster sugar, for glazing

filling
550g (about 3) Granny Smith or tart apples
1 Tbsp lemon juice
500g rhubarb, trimmed and sliced
110g caster sugar, plus extra for dredging
2 Tbsp cornflour
¼ tsp ground cinnamon

for serving
custard, cream or ice cream

1 Have ready a 20cm enamel pie plate, and centre a pie bird in the middle so steam can escape.

2 To make the pastry, sift flour, salt and sugar together. Put flour mixture and butter in the bowl of a food processor fitted with the chopping blade. Process briefly until the mixture resembles coarse breadcrumbs (see cooking class on page 58). Mix egg yolk and 4 tablespoons water together and pour into the processor through the feed tube. Pulse until mixture gathers in large clumps. If you don't have a food processor, put flour, sugar and salt in a large mixing bowl and cut the butter through the flour using two knives or a pastry blender, then rub in with the fingers until it resembles coarse crumbs. Add the egg yolk mixed with 5 tablespoons of water and mix to a dough. Tip dough onto a dry, lightly floured surface and knead until smooth. Wrap in plastic food wrap and refrigerate for 30 minutes.

3 Roll out the pastry on a lightly floured surface, then transfer to a baking sheet and refrigerate while preparing filling.

4 Preheat oven to 200°C (regular bake). Peel apples, cut into quarters and remove cores. Slice thinly. Put apples in a bowl with lemon juice and toss gently until coated. Add rhubarb, then sugar, cornflour and cinnamon and toss gently. Pile fruit into pie plate – there is a lot of fruit, but it will collapse as it cooks, so pile it up around the pie bird and press gently to get rid of as much air as possible.

5 Cut a long strip of pastry from rolled-out dough. Dampen rim of pie dish and press pastry strip onto it, then dampen the top of the pastry strip with water. Cut a cross in the centre of the remaining piece of pastry and drape it over the fruit, letting the pie bird pop through the cut in the centre. Seal pastry edges, trim, then crimp edges with the fingers. Roll out the pastry scraps and cut into leaves and other decorative pieces. Attach to the pastry with a little milk.

6 Brush pastry top with milk and sprinkle with sugar. Put pie plate on a baking sheet (I usually encase the bottom of the pie plate in tin foil to catch any juices that may spill out during cooking – it makes for easy cleaning). Bake for 30 minutes until golden, then drape the pie with tin foil and continue cooking for a further 15 minutes. Serve hot or warm with custard, cream or ice cream.

blueberry tart

ready in 45 minutes, plus chilling | serves 6–8

This is an ideal dessert for those who love pastry but hate making it. Simply buy a block of pastry, roll it out, line it into a flan ring, fill it with a quickly made creamy filling and strew with blueberries. Gorgeous!

400g ready-made sweet shortcrust pastry, or a batch made with 225g standard flour (page 52)
125g mascarpone
70ml sour cream
finely grated zest of 1 lemon
2 tsp caster sugar
⅛ tsp ground cinnamon
375g fresh blueberries
icing sugar, for dusting

1 Preheat oven to 180°C (fanbake). Have ready a 23cm loose-bottomed flan ring set on a baking sheet lined with baking paper.

2 Roll out pastry and line into flan ring. Prick pastry all over with a fork, then chill for 30 minutes. Line pastry with tin foil and baking beans and bake blind for 15 minutes (see cooking class on page 83). Remove foil and beans and return pastry to oven to cook for 10–15 minutes more, or until golden. Cool.

3 Beat the mascarpone, sour cream, lemon zest, sugar and cinnamon together in a bowl. Spread this mixture over pastry, and pile blueberries on top. Dust with icing sugar and serve cut into slices.

chiffon pie

ready in 1 hour 15 minutes, plus chilling | serves 8

If you want to use homemade pastry for this dessert, make a batch with 225g standard flour, sweetening it with 1 tablespoon caster sugar (see page 52). There will be quite a bit left over. Re-roll and cut out rounds with a pastry cutter and freeze in a container or sealable bag, then you'll have pastries on hand for small quiches or tartlets.

350g ready-made sweet shortcrust pastry

1 Tbsp water

1 tsp powdered gelatine

2 medium (size 6) free-range eggs, at room temperature

75g caster sugar

finely grated zest and strained juice of 1 lemon

pinch of salt

50ml cream, lightly whipped, plus extra for serving

strawberries, hulled and sliced, to serve

caster sugar, for strawberries (optional)

1 Preheat oven to 190°C (fanbake). Have a 20cm flan ring ready, set on a baking sheet lined with baking paper.

2 Roll out the pastry and line into flan ring. Chill until firm. Line with tin foil, then fill with baking beans. Blind-bake pastry until crisp and golden (see cooking class on page 83). Homemade pastry will need 25 minutes, then remove foil and beans and return to oven for 2–3 minutes until golden. Ready-made pastry takes a little less time, 20–25 minutes, then remove foil and beans and return to oven for a few minutes more to dry the top of the pastry. Cool.

3 Put water in a ramekin and sprinkle the gelatine over. Put the ramekin in a small heatproof dish of warm water and transfer to an element over a very gentle heat. Stir until the gelatine is dissolved and the liquid is clear.

4 Separate eggs, putting whites in a grease-free bowl and yolks in a Pyrex or china bowl. Beat yolks with 50g of the sugar, the lemon juice and pinch of salt. Put the bowl over a small saucepan of gently simmering water and whisk mixture with a hand-held electric beater until thick and mousse-like. Remove bowl from the hot water, add lemon zest and dissolved gelatine. Continue whisking until light and fluffy and on the point of setting.

5 Fold whipped cream into lemon and egg yolks. Whisk whites with remaining sugar until stiff (but don't beat them as stiff as for a meringue), and fold into the chiffon mixture. Pile mixture into the pastry case, smooth the top and chill. Serve with strawberries, sprinkled with sugar if liked, and lightly whipped cream.

A cooking class with Julie

Rich shortcrust pastry

Traditional English shortcrust pastry uses half the amount of fat to the flour. Water is used for mixing. Rich shortcrust pastry has a higher ratio of fat to flour, usually three-quarters fat to flour, making it flakier, more tender and 'shorter' in texture – more melt-in-the-mouth and easier to cut – and egg yolk is mixed with the water to enrich the pastry. Both pastries can be used for pies, flans, tarts and tartlets. The recipes in this book call for rich shortcrust.

My preference is for butter (not lard and butter; and never margarine, as I prefer a natural product and do not use margarine) and all-purpose standard flour. The butter should be cool but pliable, not set hard, or it will not blend properly with the flour. For sweet pastry, a little caster sugar is added to sweeten the dough and give a nice crisp finish. Unsalted butter is preferable, as it is hard to tell how much salt there is in salted butter. A little salt is sifted with the flour to flavour the dough.

1

If you are following an English recipe and making it with flour milled in New Zealand or Australia, you will most likely need to increase the amount of liquid called for because the flours are milled differently. Antipodean standard flours seem to be drier than those in the UK (the finer the flour, the more liquid it will absorb).

Tarts and flans with soggy pastry on the bottom are a disappointment, but there is much you can do to prevent this happening. A metal flan ring placed on a baking sheet produces a crisper base to the pastry, as excess moisture from the filling can escape from underneath the flan ring in the form of steam. In a china flan dish the moisture is trapped and can cause the pastry to become soggy. Loose-bottomed flan rings also produce a good result. The flan ring can easily be slipped off after baking, leaving the flan supported on the metal base. Metal is also a better conductor of heat than china.

And here's another great tip: cover one baking sheet with baking paper and have a second baking sheet heating in the oven. Line the pastry into the flan ring on the baking paper, then slide paper and pastry straight onto the hot baking sheet. This gives a burst of bottom heat to help get the cooking underway.

2

Making rich shortcrust pastry by hand

Work in a cool kitchen. Use a large, wide bowl; a tall or narrow bowl will restrict movement and make it difficult to rub the butter into the flour. Sift flour, salt and sugar (if using) into bowl to aerate. Cut butter into cubes and drop into flour. Use two round-bladed knives (picture 1) to cut the butter through the flour. The metal knives keep the fat cool. Alternatively, use a metal pastry blender (see page 82, picture 2). Then finish rubbing in the butter with the fingertips. The further up your hand you go the warmer it becomes, so use fingertips only. As you rub the butter into the flour, lift it slightly in the bowl to keep it aerated (picture 2). This makes the pastry light. Shake the bowl occasionally to bring the larger lumps of butter to the surface (picture 3). Once the mixture looks like coarse breadcrumbs, stop. The idea is to get the butter coated with flour, not to have the flour absorb the butter. These pieces of butter will disperse through the dough when rolled but will help create little air pockets during baking which will make the pastry flaky. If you overwork the ingredients at this stage, the pastry will be heavy and greasy.

3

4

5

6

Blend egg yolk and chilled water together and mix into flour and butter with a knife, working quickly but lightly (picture 4). Once it starts to form a clumpy ball, use your hand to bring it to a smooth ball, but use minimum and light contact (picture 5). If you move the ball of clumpy dough around the bowl it should start to look clean. If there are a lot of floury flakes, as in picture 6, dribble in a little more water. If the dough is too dry, it will be flaky and difficult to roll and shape, and is likely to crack. Conversely, if the dough is sticky or wet it will be difficult to handle and may be hard and tough when baked, and may shrink.

Making rich shortcrust pastry in a food processor

Pastry can be made successfully in a food processor. It requires less water than when making by hand (4 tablespoons to 225g standard flour), and care must be taken not to overwork the dough or it will become oily.

Sift flour, salt and sugar (if using) together, then transfer to the bowl of a food processor fitted with the chopping blade. Add butter and process briefly until the mixture resembles coarse breadcrumbs. Mix egg yolk and chilled water together and pour all of it into the processor. Pulse just until mixture gathers in large clumps (picture 1), then turn it out and use your hands to gather into a smooth ball (pictures 2 to 4).

1

2

3

4

Rolling out pastry

Rest the dough before rolling. This will make it more manageable, easier to roll, and less inclined to shrink during cooking. Wrap it in plastic food wrap and refrigerate for about 30 minutes until firm. Do not let it become hard or it will be difficult to roll; if this happens, let it soften a little at room temperature before rolling.

Marble or a cool surface is ideal for rolling out pastry. The aim is to keep the pastry cool during rolling to prevent butter bursting through and making the pastry sticky. Use a long wooden rolling pin. Wipe rolling pin clean after use; never soak it in water or it will swell and become uneven.

Flour the pin not the pastry, or you will roll in an unnecessary amount of flour that could make the pastry dry (picture 1). You want just enough to stop sticking – dab any patches with a little flour if necessary. Roll in one direction only, releasing the pressure from the pin on the return of the roll. This prevents stretching the pastry and having it shrink during cooking. Keep moving the pastry to ensure it is not catching on the surface. To flour underneath the pastry, don't turn the pastry over (this could stretch it); just move it to another part of the work bench, sprinkle bench with a little flour, then move the pastry back to the floured area.

1

2

3

To roll out a round shape, which is easier to line into a round flan ring and saves wastage, think of the pastry like a clock. After each roll, turn the pastry clockwise by 2 hours (pictures 2 and 3).

The pastry can also be rolled between baking paper or plastic food wrap when making pastries with a high fat content such as nut pastry, or when making pastry in humid conditions. It is also an especially good tip for novice cooks.

If pastry has warmed up and feels limp after rolling, put it on a baking sheet and chill until firm.

Lining into a flan ring

Do not grease the flan ring, as the pastry will slip off it as it cooks. Put flan ring on a baking sheet lined with baking paper.

Gently roll pastry around rolling pin – don't drape it or it will stretch, which can cause it to shrink during cooking (picture 1, opposite). Gently brush off any excess flour (which can make the pastry dry and caked).

Gently unroll pastry over the flan ring (picture 2), then ease it into the ring, pressing it right into the corners, and letting the pastry settle in without stretching or pulling (pictures 3 and 4). If fingers are warm or dough is a little sticky, coat fingers in flour first; or roll a small lump of dough into a ball, coat it in flour and use it to push the pastry into place. At no time stretch or pull the pastry, as this can cause it to shrink during cooking.

Let excess pastry drape over edge of flan ring. If sides of pastry are cut even with the flan ring, the pastry will shrink down during cooking. If the filling contains eggs, the filling may puff up and could flow over the top and down the sides of the flan ring; this could result in a loss of filling and burning on the bottom of the oven, or the tart or pie could stick to the ring as it cools. Here's the trick: as you roll the pin over the top of the flan ring it pushes a little of the pastry back into the ring (pictures 5 and 6). Use this to form a ledge. Roll off excess pastry with the pin, then go around with the fingers and thumb and form the ledge of pastry. This will rise up with the filling and prevent the filling from running over the top of pastry. As the filling cools the pastry ledge settles back into place.

If the filling is quite a firm, solid mixture, prick the pastry base before putting in the filling. If the mixture is liquid, as in a custard, prick it after 15 minutes of cooking – not before or it may ooze out. Pricking prevents air getting trapped between the pastry and the paper-lined baking sheet, which can cause hollows of uncooked pastry.

Before baking, the pastry must be well chilled. If it has warmed up during lining, chill it until firm. If you put soft, limp pastry into a hot oven, the butter or fat will melt before the flour has time to cook and the pastry will collapse down the sides of the flan ring. If the pastry is chilled until the fat is hard and cold, the flour will have time to cook first. The starch grains can then pop with the heat, swell a little and embrace the particles of fat so they can't run off. The pastry then stays in position.

1

2

3

4

5

6

special occasions

raspberry brûlée spoons

ready in 30 minutes, plus chilling | makes 12–16 spoons

These little mouthfuls look as cute as a button and are just the trick for a sweet and stylish end to a soirée where plates and cutlery are too cumbersome. However, they can also be made in six to eight small ramekins instead of spoons.

1 Fill a shallow tin, such as a Swiss roll tin, with large cubes of ice. Set the spoons on top of the ice and put a raspberry in each. The ice will prevent the custard from curdling while the sugar is caramelised.

2 To make the custard, beat egg yolks and caster sugar together in a small bowl for 2–3 minutes until pale and smooth. Put cream in a saucepan, scrape in seeds from vanilla pod, and add the pod too. Bring cream to a gentle boil, then pour 2–3 tablespoons of cream onto the yolks. Blend well, then pour the egg mixture into the pan of cream.

3 Cook custard over a low to medium heat, stirring constantly with a wooden spoon until the custard thickens and coats the back of the spoon (see cooking class on page 84). On no account let the custard reach boiling point or it will curdle. Remove vanilla pod (the vanilla pod can be washed, left to dry and reused).

4 Pour custard over the raspberries in the spoons, filling the spoons right to the top.

5 Sprinkle caster sugar over top of custards and use a small culinary blowtorch to caramelise the sugar. I do not suggest attempting to grill these under an oven grill. The brûlée spoons can be served straightaway (they're a bit harder to eat when crunchy, but are manageable). Alternatively, chill them for a few hours (or overnight for a softer finish) before serving.

12–16 Chinese spoons
12–16 fresh raspberries

custard
2 medium (size 6) free-range egg yolks
2½ Tbsp caster sugar, plus extra for sprinkling
300ml cream
small vanilla pod, split

rhubarb brûlée

ready in 25 minutes, plus chilling | serves 4

These desserts need to be prepared ahead, which makes them a good choice for a dinner party. For a change, use redcurrant jelly and a little orange juice in place of the sugar when cooking the rhubarb. Serve any remaining rhubarb juices over cereal for breakfast.

400g rhubarb
75g caster sugar

custard
2 medium (size 6) free-range egg yolks
30g caster sugar
300ml cream
½ vanilla pod, split
4 Tbsp caster or demerara sugar

1 Preheat oven to 180°C (fanbake).

2 Wash and trim rhubarb and cut into short lengths. Put rhubarb in a shallow baking dish and sprinkle with sugar. Cover with tin foil and bake for 15–20 minutes, or until just tender (after 15 minutes' cooking time, check rhubarb every minute because it quickly blows open and turns to mush). Transfer to a large sieve to drain, reserving juices.

3 To make the custard, whisk egg yolks and the first measure of sugar together in a small bowl until thick and pale. Put cream in a saucepan and scrape in seeds from vanilla pod, then add the pod too. Bring cream to a gentle boil, then pour 2–3 tablespoons of cream onto the egg yolks. Blend well, then tip yolks and sugar into the pan of cream.

4 Cook custard over a medium heat, stirring constantly with a wooden spoon until custard thickens and coats the spoon (see cooking class on page 84). Do not let custard boil, or it will curdle. Remove vanilla pod (the vanilla pod can be washed, left to dry and reused).

5 Divide rhubarb among four ramekins, or small teacups or coffee cups, and pour over hot custard. Put ramekins or cups in a shallow container, cool, then refrigerate overnight.

6 Sprinkle caster or demerara sugar over top of custards and use a small culinary blowtorch to glaze them, or glaze under a preheated grill, until the sugar caramelises. This is best done quickly to avoid the custard heating and separating. Immediately remove from heat and chill again for a few hours before serving.

gingerbreads with baby pears

ready in 1 hour | makes 12

Whole baby canned pears are so cute! They're available from specialist food stores. I make these gingerbreads in small moulds, just a step up in size from dariole moulds, and I sometimes use a Tupperware baking mould. If you only have six moulds, cook them in two batches. The gingerbreads are just as good a day after making. If canned baby whole pears are not available, use small whole pears, such as honey belle, poached.

170g brown sugar

125g butter

75g golden syrup

120g black treacle

330g standard flour

1 heaped tsp ground ginger

¼ tsp salt

1½ tsp baking powder

1 medium (size 6) free-range egg

300ml milk

1 tsp baking soda dissolved in a
   little milk

12 whole baby canned pears,
   drained and patted dry

icing sugar, for dusting

cream or homemade custard
   (page 97), for serving

1 Preheat oven to 175°C (regular bake).

2 Warm the sugar, butter, golden syrup and black treacle in a small saucepan until butter is melted and sugar is dissolved (don't boil), then cool for several minutes.

3 Sift flour, ginger, salt and baking powder together into a large bowl. Make a well in the centre. Beat egg and milk together. Add to dry ingredients with the baking soda dissolved in milk. Mix until combined, but don't beat.

4 Bake puddings in small moulds. Pour a little of the mixture into each mould, then drop in a pear, and top up with batter until the pear is just covered; the moulds should be about three-quarters full. Bake for about 35 minutes until browned on top and slightly springy when pressed lightly with the finger. Cool puddings in the moulds for 10 minutes, then turn them onto a cooling rack. Dust with icing sugar and serve with a little cream or custard.

hazelnut meringue gâteau

ready in 1 hour 35 minutes, plus cooling | serves 8–10

This is one of the most glorious meringue gâteaux ever. The toasted hazelnuts give an almost coffee-like aroma and flavour, and the meringue, after softening a little with cream, is crisp on the top and tender in the centre, with the welcome crunch of nuts. Yum beyond belief!

125g hazelnuts

4 medium (size 6) free-range egg whites, at room temperature

250g caster sugar

¼ tsp vanilla extract

½ tsp white vinegar

200ml cream

300g raspberries

icing sugar, for dusting

1 Preheat oven to 180°C (regular bake). Line the bases and sides of two shallow 20cm sandwich tins, preferably loose-bottomed, with baking paper.

2 Put hazelnuts in a shallow ovenproof dish and bake for about 12 minutes, or until lightly golden. The skins should start peeling back and the nuts will have started to colour. Tip nuts onto a clean cloth, bundle up and rub vigorously to release the skins. Reduce oven temperature to 170°C.

3 Grind nuts in a food processor, just until they are finely chopped – don't process them too long or they'll turn oily. Set aside.

4 Whisk egg whites with an electric beater until stiff, then beat in the caster sugar a little at a time and continue whisking until stiff and glossy (see cooking class on page 134). Sprinkle vanilla extract and vinegar over, whisk for 10 seconds, then turn off the machine. Scatter the hazelnuts over the meringue and fold them in carefully using a large metal spoon, being careful not to deflate the meringue.

5 Divide mixture between prepared tins. Bake for about 40 minutes or until very crisp on top. Cool in the tins for 10 minutes, then remove from tins and peel off paper. Cool completely, then store in an airtight container for up to 48 hours.

6 To finish off, whip the cream until thick and just holding its shape. Put one round of meringue on a large plate or cake stand (put a few dabs of cream underneath the meringue to stop it from sliding around). Spoon the cream on top, then add half the raspberries and sandwich together with the other meringue round. Put the rest of the raspberries on top and dust with icing sugar. Refrigerate for 2–3 hours before serving to soften the meringue a little and make it easy to slice into portions.

vanilla sugar mango tarts with caramel sauce

ready in just over 2 hours | makes 8

These tarts make an impressive end to a knock-your-socks-off dinner party, but allow plenty of time to make the caramel, and make the pastry first while the kitchen is cool.

caramel sauce
395g can sweetened condensed milk

plain unsweetened yoghurt, to serve

rich shortcrust pastry
225g standard flour

pinch of salt

170g unsalted butter, firm but pliable

1 medium (size 6) free-range egg yolk

4–5 Tbsp chilled water

fruit
2 large, perfectly ripe, unblemished mangoes

vanilla-scented raw sugar, or raw sugar plus a liberal sprinkle of seeds scraped from a piece of vanilla pod

1 To make the caramel sauce, put the unopened can of condensed milk in a saucepan, pour in water up to the rim of the can and boil gently for 2 hours. Top up with boiling water from the kettle every 20 minutes or so. Cool. Open can carefully. Scrape contents of can into a bowl and beat until smooth. Before serving, mix in enough yoghurt to bring it to a pouring consistency.

2 To make the pastry, sift flour with salt. Put butter and flour in the bowl of a food processor fitted with the chopping blade. Process briefly until the mixture resembles coarse breadcrumbs (see cooking class on page 58). Mix egg yolk and 4 tablespoons water together and pour into the processor through the feed tube. Pulse just until dough gathers in clumps. If you don't have a food processor, put flour and salt in a large mixing bowl and cut the butter through the flour using two knives or a pastry blender, then rub in with the fingers until it resembles coarse crumbs. Add the egg yolk mixed with 5 tablespoons of water and mix to a dough. Tip dough onto a dry, lightly floured surface and knead until smooth. Wrap in plastic food wrap and refrigerate for 15 minutes until just firm.

3 Preheat oven to 180°C (fanbake). Roll out pastry on a lightly floured surface and line into eight small (about 10cm), loose-bottomed metal tartlet rings (re-roll scraps if necessary). Put tartlet rings on a baking sheet and chill until pastry is firm. Line each with light tin foil and fill with baking beans. Bake blind for 15 minutes, or until pastry is set in place and has coloured around the rim. Remove foil and beans.

4 Peel mangoes and slice the flesh away from the stones, then cut into thinnish slices. Arrange mango slices in tarts. Sprinkle mango generously with vanilla sugar, then return tarts to oven for a further 12–15 minutes. Serve warm with caramel sauce.

spiced ginger roll

ready in 1 hour 15 minutes | serves 8 or more

This is a pretty stunning dessert, and not the sort of thing you whip up mid-week for the kids. Don't worry about cracks on top of the ginger roll – that's normal – but do take care not to overcook the sponge, keeping it soft and moist and not letting it get dry and leathery. Cooking apples with the skin and pips saves wastage, and gives the purée more flavour and a thicker consistency.

1 Preheat oven to 175°C (regular bake). Line a 23cm × 30cm Swiss roll tin with baking paper, folding it at the corners to make a neat paper case (see cooking class on page 165).

2 To make the apple purée, cut apples into thick chunks and put them in a saucepan with the butter and water. Cover pan with a lid and cook very gently for 15–20 minutes, or until very tender. Rub apples through a sieve, discarding skin and pips. Return purée to a clean pan and cook gently for 5–10 minutes, stirring often, until thick and somewhat reduced. Sweeten purée to taste with caster sugar.

3 To make the sponge, sift flour, salt and spices together into a large bowl. Warm golden syrup, treacle and butter in a small saucepan until butter has melted (see cooking class on page 165). Whisk egg, add water and baking soda, then pour into the dry ingredients. Mix together, then pour melted syrup mixture in. Whisk lightly for 30 seconds. Pour into the prepared Swiss roll tin.

4 Bake sponge for about 15 minutes, until browned and springy to the touch. Turn out onto a large piece of greaseproof or baking paper dusted with icing sugar. Spread sponge with a thin layer of jam, then one of apple purée. Trim edges and roll up, using the paper as support. Dust the top with caster sugar and serve hot as a dessert with extra apple purée and hot custard, if liked.

apple purée

800g (about 4 large) Granny Smith or other tart apples, washed
½ tsp butter
1 Tbsp water
about 1 Tbsp caster sugar

sponge

120g standard flour
pinch of salt
1 level tsp each ground cinnamon, mixed spice, nutmeg and ginger
2 Tbsp golden syrup
2 Tbsp black treacle
75g unsalted butter
1 medium (size 6) free-range egg
125ml warm water
1 tsp baking soda

to finish

icing sugar, for dusting
1–2 Tbsp plum jam
caster sugar, for dusting
homemade custard (page 97), for serving (optional)

honey and vanilla cheesecakes

ready in 50 minutes, plus cooling | makes 6

Quark is a soft, white moist cheese with a fresh lemony tang. It's more subtle than plain unsweetened yoghurt or cream cheese, and does not have the firm curd of cottage cheese. It has the advantage of blending smoothly with other ingredients. If made with skimmed milk it has less than around 2% fat, but if made with whole milk the fat content may be as high as 10% (which is still lower than many other milk products).

100g digestive biscuits

30g butter, melted

3 medium (size 6) free-range eggs

360g quark

½ tsp vanilla extract

90ml liquid honey

2 Tbsp raw sugar

finely grated zest of 1 orange

250g strawberries, hulled and sliced

1 Tbsp icing sugar, plus extra for dusting

1 Tbsp fresh orange juice

1 Preheat oven to 160°C (regular bake). Line the bottoms of six ramekins with a disc of baking paper.

2 Break biscuits into the bowl of a food processor and process to fine crumbs. Alternatively, put biscuits in a large sealable bag and crush with a rolling pin. Pour in melted butter and mix briefly. Divide between ramekins and press crumbs into the bottom of each.

3 Break the eggs into a bowl, beat with a small whisk, then whisk in the quark, vanilla extract, honey and sugar and whisk until smooth. Pass the mixture through a coarse sieve into a bowl to catch the chalzae (chords) of the eggs (discard these to ensure velvety smooth cheesecakes), and blend in the orange zest. Put ramekins in a shallow ovenproof tin (like a Swiss roll tin) to make it easier to take them in and out of the oven, and pour in filling.

4 Bake for about 30–35 minutes, or until the filling is set, with just a hint of a wobble. Cool for 1 hour, loosen from the sides of the ramekins, then invert onto serving plates. Peel off discs of paper.

5 Mix the strawberries, icing sugar and orange juice together in a bowl. Dust cheesecakes with icing sugar and serve with the strawberries.

prune and frangipane tart

ready in 1 hour, plus cooling | serves 10

This is the perfect dessert to end a spectacular winter dinner.

sweet rich shortcrust pastry

225g standard flour

pinch of salt

1 Tbsp caster sugar

150g unsalted butter, firm but pliable

1 medium (size 6) free-range egg yolk, at room temperature

4–5 Tbsp chilled water

filling

175g pitted prunes

2 Tbsp brandy or cognac

3 Tbsp water

200g unsalted butter, softened

200g caster sugar

2 large (size 7) free-range eggs, plus 2 large egg yolks

210g ground almonds

4 Tbsp standard flour

glaze

150ml apricot jam, warmed and sifted

1 Tbsp lemon juice

1 To make the pastry, sift flour, salt and sugar together, then transfer to the bowl of a food processor fitted with the chopping blade. Add butter and process briefly until the mixture resembles coarse breadcrumbs (see cooking class on page 58). Mix egg yolk and 4 tablespoons of water together and pour into the processor through the feed tube. Pulse until mixture gathers in large clumps. If you don't have a food processor, put flour, sugar and salt in a large mixing bowl and cut the butter through the flour using two knives or a pastry blender, then rub in with the fingers until it resembles coarse crumbs. Add the egg yolk mixed with 5 tablespoons of water and mix to a dough. Tip dough onto a dry, lightly floured surface and knead until smooth. Wrap in plastic food wrap and refrigerate for 30 minutes.

2 Preheat oven to 180°C (fanbake). Roll out pastry into a large round (see page 60) on lightly floured baking paper. Have ready a 30cm loose-bottomed flan tin set on a baking sheet lined with baking paper. Have another baking sheet heating in the bottom third of the oven. Turn pastry into flan tin, push it gently into the edges of the tin, then peel off the paper. Roll off excess pastry. Prick base with a fork. Chill until firm.

3 Line pastry with light tin foil and fill with baking beans. Slide flan and paper off cold baking sheet onto heated sheet. Bake for 20 minutes, or until pastry is set in place and has coloured around the rim.

4 Put prunes in a small saucepan with brandy and water, cover and set pan on a very low heat. Simmer gently for 10 minutes, making sure the water doesn't evaporate.

5 To make the frangipane, whip butter and sugar together in a food processor until light and fluffy. Scrape down the sides of the bowl. With the machine running, gradually whip in the whole eggs and egg yolks, then the ground almonds and flour. Spoon frangipane into partially cooked pastry case and spread it out evenly with a knife. Dot with prunes, pressing them to the bottom of the pastry. Bake for about 30 minutes, or until frangipane is golden brown and set and the pastry is cooked. Transfer to a cooling rack and cool for 10 minutes.

6 Heat apricot jam and lemon juice in a small saucepan. Dissolve gently, then bring to a bubble. Brush hot glaze over surface of tart. Leave dessert to cool before removing from flan tin.

strawberry butterfly cakes

ready in 45 minutes, plus cooling | makes about 18

These are so cute, and are loved by all generations – kids, grannies and in-betweens. They're best eaten the day they are made while they're soft and fresh. And, regarding strawberries, it pays to be fussy when buying them or other berries. Always check the bottom of the punnet to make sure there is no juice (juice indicates the strawberries have been squashed or are over-ripe). Pale-coloured strawberries have most likely been picked before they were fully ripe – they won't ripen any further. The juiciest and tastiest strawberries are those grown in warm, dry spring or early summer weather, before it gets too hot and humid.

125g unsalted butter, cubed and
softened

115g caster sugar

2 medium (size 6) free-range eggs,
at room temperature

120g standard flour

2 tsp baking powder

60ml milk

½ tsp vanilla extract

icing sugar, for dusting

strawberry conserve or jam

200ml cream, lightly whipped

fresh strawberries, hulled and
sliced, for filling

1 Preheat oven to 180°C (regular bake). Set 18 paper cases inside muffin tins.

2 Put butter in a bowl and beat with an electric beater until creamy and loose, then gradually beat in caster sugar and continue beating until fluffy and lighter in colour (creamed; see cooking class on page 111). You'll need to stop the machine and scrape down the sides of the bowl several times. Beat eggs together with a fork, then add them gradually to the creamed butter and sugar, adding 2 tablespoons of the measured flour halfway through beating to help stabilise the mixture.

3 Sift remaining flour and baking powder together onto a piece of paper, then sift them over the creamed butter and eggs. Fold in with a large spoon, then mix in the milk and vanilla extract.

4 Scoop up the mixture with a teaspoon and use another teaspoon to push mixture into a paper case. When all are done, bake for 15 minutes, or until the cakes are an even, light golden brown and springy to the touch. Cool cakes in the paper cases on a cooling rack.

5 Just before serving, cut a small disc from the top of each sponge cake (discard these bits or eat them!). Dust tops of cupcakes with icing sugar. Put a dollop of strawberry conserve or jam in the holes, then cover with a dollop of lightly whipped cream. Arrange strawberry slices in the cream to make butterfly wings. Serve immediately.

exotic fruit salad

ready in 20 minutes | serves 6

This salad is a blend of summer's gorgeous fruit given an exotic touch with a dash of muscatel vinegar. The sweet grapey and fruity perfume of muscat grapes gives the vinegar immediate appeal – it is totally seductive and, I warn you, addictive. Muscatel vinegar is also excellent in trifles and creamy desserts, or with savoury dishes with duck, chicken, pork and turkey. If you are unable to find it, try another type of fruit vinegar such as raspberry, strawberry, feijoa or peach. You could also substitute verjuice or vincotto to taste.

1kg wedge watermelon
4 white or yellow nectarines or peaches
2 plums
150g small, crunchy red grapes
150g cherries
1 large wedge fresh pineapple
2 Tbsp muscatel vinegar
3 Tbsp vanilla sugar

1 Peel, pip, slice or prepare fruit as appropriate. Put all fruit in a large bowl and chill until required (up to 1 hour).

2 In a small bowl, blend muscatel vinegar and vanilla sugar together. Pour over fruit, toss gently and serve immediately.

melting moments with passionfruit cream

ready in 1 hour | makes about 30

These melt-in-the-mouth biscuits will keep fresh and crisp for some days in an airtight container. Fill them with passionfruit cream just before serving.

biscuits
250g unsalted butter, at room temperature
80g icing sugar
¼ tsp vanilla extract
210g standard flour
pinch of salt
100g cornflour

passionfruit cream
100g mascarpone
1 tsp caster sugar
1 large or 2 small passionfruit

1 Preheat oven to 180°C (regular bake).

2 Put butter in a warmed bowl and beat with an electric beater until creamy and loose. Add icing sugar and vanilla and beat until light in colour (creamed; see cooking class on page 111), stopping the machine and scraping down the sides of the bowl several times.

3 Sift flour, salt and cornflour together, and stir into the creamed mixture. Roll dough into small balls and put on a baking sheet lined with baking paper. Press each lightly with a floured fork.

4 Bake biscuits for about 15 minutes until firm and lightly golden; don't over-cook. Cool on the baking sheet for 5 minutes, then transfer to a cooling rack to cool further.

5 Mix mascarpone, sugar and passionfruit pulp together in a small bowl. Sandwich biscuits together with passionfruit cream and serve.

A cooking class with Julie

Using the rubbing-in method

The rubbing-in method of cake making is probably the easiest and most forgiving. It is used for plainer cakes, often those based on an economical list of ingredients, and for scones, rock cakes and coffee buns. The same technique is also used for making shortcrust and rich shortcrust pastry, and crumble toppings. Cakes and scones made with this method are best consumed the day of baking, or at most within two days, because they are low in fat and sugar – two ingredients which keep baking tender and moist – and their texture dries quickly.

1

2

Sift flour, a pinch of salt and any spices called for in the recipe into a wide bowl. Cut butter into cubes, add to dry ingredients and cut into the flour using two round-bladed knives (picture 1). This keeps your fingers and hands off the butter. The aim is to get the butter mixed through the dry ingredients without it warming too much, because if the butter turns oily it will make the texture heavy. Alternatively, use a pastry blender (picture 2).

3

Shake the bowl from time to time to bring big lumps to the top so you can see how much further you need to go (see page 58, picture 3). Once the pieces are about the size of green peas, use your fingers to finish the job. Rub the butter through the flour by picking it up with your fingers and letting it slip through fingers and thumbs while gently pressing it together (picture 3). Working at a height keeps the mixture aerated and light, a job that is difficult to do in a narrow bowl. Stop once the mixture looks like coarse breadcrumbs and continue with the recipe.

To compensate for fruit sinking in a crumble during cooking, fill a ramekin or other dish with fruit to come just under the top of the rim, then mound the crumble on top (picture 4). The crumble will sink down with the fruit during cooking, but when cooked it will still look generously full, instead of sunken and sad. A little gap around the edge of the crumble will allow steam from the fuit to escape.

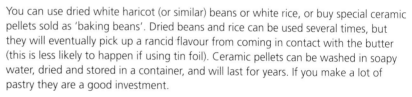

4

Blind-baking pastry

Unbaked pastry cases can be filled and baked, or the pastry case can be partially baked before putting in the filling. To partially bake a pastry case, it is first lined with soft paper or tin foil and weighted with baking beans, then cooked for a short while. This is known as 'baking blind' – the term simply means that the pastry is hidden by the paper as it cooks. It's a technique that is very helpful when cooking in an oven that does not have good bottom heat, or for flans, tarts and pies with moist fillings, as it helps avoid a soggy bottom. If the pastry case is to be filled with fresh fruit, a filling that doesn't require cooking, or one that is already cooked, the pastry can be cooked right through (the beans and lining are removed for the last few minutes of cooking).

You can use dried white haricot (or similar) beans or white rice, or buy special ceramic pellets sold as 'baking beans'. Dried beans and rice can be used several times, but they will eventually pick up a rancid flavour from coming in contact with the butter (this is less likely to happen if using tin foil). Ceramic pellets can be washed in soapy water, dried and stored in a container, and will last for years. If you make a lot of pastry they are a good investment.

To bake blind, line the pastry case with white tissue paper or soft tin foil (stiff, heavy-duty foil can tear the pastry). Put in the baking beans. The paper or foil helps support the pastry until it is cooked into shape, and the baking beans hold the paper down (picture 1). In my experience, it is not necessary to fill the pastry case to the top with baking beans providing the pastry is well chilled (although some books will tell you to do so); you only need enough beans to weigh down the bottom of the pastry, as the paper or foil will support the sides.

1

To partially blind-bake a pastry case, bake for 15–20 minutes in an oven preheated to 180°C (fanbake). If your oven doesn't have good bottom heat, cook pies, flans and tarts in the bottom third of the oven and experiment with temperature, increasing it to 190°C (fanbake). If you don't have a fanbake option on your oven, cook at 200°C.

To completely blind-bake a pastry case, allow 25–30 minutes, or until pastry is golden and shows no greasy patches. Remove the baking beans and paper or foil for the final 5 or so minutes to ensure the pastry is thoroughly baked.

Making custard

Crème à la vanille sounds impressive but it is simply a French name describing English soft or pouring custard flavoured with vanilla. To make it, vanilla seeds and pod are added to whole milk (picture 1), and the milk is heated until hand-hot and left to infuse. Egg yolks and sugar are beaten together with a wooden spoon until the yolks become a little paler in colour. 2–3 tablespoons of the infused milk is poured onto the eggs and sugar and blended well (picture 2), then the lot is poured back into the saucepan and stirred over a very gentle heat until thick and creamy.

At first the mixture will be thin and frothy, and if you run your finger down the back of the wooden spoon, it will barely leave an impression (picture 3). Once the custard has thickened, the impression will be easily visible (picture 4).

If the heat is too high the custard will curdle (go lumpy) so it must not boil. The key to a smooth, creamy custard is gentle heat and constant stirring. If the heat gets away on you and the custard starts to curdle, immediately remove pan from heat, immerse bottom of pan in a sink of cold water and beat the custard vigorously. You may be lucky. To help prevent curdling when making custard with milk, add a small amount of arrowroot to the eggs and sugar (1 level teaspoon per 3 medium [size 6] egg yolks). If making custard with cream, the arrowroot can be omitted.

1

2

3

4

5

6

7

As soon as the custard is ready, remove pan from heat and pour custard into a bowl (picture 5). If you wish to remove the flecks of vanilla, strain the custard through a fine sieve. The custard will form a skin as it cools; to prevent this, sprinkle the top of the custard with caster sugar (picture 6).

Custard made as described can be served with desserts, as you would cream or ice cream, or it can be incorporated into desserts, such as tiramisu, trifles, cold soufflés and ice creams. Other flavourings, such as the zest of orange, lemon or lime, crushed coffee beans and chocolate can be infused with the milk, then strained off.

Baked custards generally require a proportion of egg white to help them set (2 whole eggs and 2 yolks will set 300ml of whole milk). If 4 whole eggs were used, the mixture would be unpleasantly firm and would have a greater tendency to curdle. (Petits pots de crème [page 131] are made with 3 whole eggs, 3 egg yolks and 450ml milk.) A thick china dish will offer some protection to a baked custard, but immersing the dish in a bain marie (an ovenproof dish or pan half-filled with hot water) is a safer option (picture 7), and helps prevent custards overheating and curdling.

comfort

lemon delicious

ready in 1 hour | serves 6

This pudding – a soft buttery sponge with crusty edge and a gooey custardy bottom – is aptly named.

1 Preheat oven to 170°C (regular bake).

2 Put butter in a large bowl and briefly beat with an electric beater until creamy and loose. Beat in caster sugar a tablespoon at a time and continue beating until fluffy and lighter in colour (creamed; see cooking class on page 111), stopping the machine and scraping the sides of the bowl down several times. Beat egg yolks together with a fork, then gradually add them to creamed butter and sugar with lemon zest, adding 2 tablespoons of the measured flour halfway through beating to help stabilise the mixture. Sift over a third of the remaining flour, fold in with a large spoon, then work in half the lemon juice. Add another third of flour, then the rest of the lemon juice, and finally the rest of the flour and the milk.

3 Whisk egg whites until soft peaks form. Work in one-third of the egg whites with a large spoon, then carefully fold in remainder (see cooking class on page 33).

4 Spoon into a 1.5-litre baking dish and bake for 30–35 minutes, or until light golden brown on top and pulling away from the sides of the dish. Serve hot or at room temperature, dusted with icing sugar and with lightly whipped cream.

75g unsalted butter, cubed then softened
175g caster sugar
3 large (size 7) free-range eggs, separated and at room temperature
finely grated zest of 3 lemons
100g self-raising flour
100ml lemon juice
175ml milk, at room temperature
icing sugar, for dusting
lightly whipped cream, to serve

brown sugar and almond crumbles with gingered apple and pear

ready in 50 minutes | serves 6

Crumbles are great served hot as a pudding with cream or ice cream, but I reckon they're better for breakfast with thick Greek yoghurt! Slice firm fruits like these apples and pears thinly, to ensure they will cook down by the time the crumble topping is ready. Don't cut back on the amount of fat in the crumble; it needs to be there to stop the crumble turning hard.

crumble

150g standard flour

120g unsalted butter, softened and cut into small pieces

3 Tbsp soft brown sugar

2 Tbsp ground almonds

finely grated zest of 1 lemon

fruit

350–400g (about 2) firm but ripe pears

400g (about 2 large) Granny Smith or other tart apples

1 Tbsp lemon juice

4 Tbsp chopped preserved ginger in syrup

1 Tbsp caster sugar

1 Preheat oven to 180°C (regular bake). Butter six ovenproof ramekins and set them in a shallow ovenproof dish in case juices bubble over during cooking.

2 To make the crumble, blend flour and butter together in a food processor until mixture resembles coarse breadcrumbs. Alternatively, cut butter into flour using two knives or a pastry blender. Transfer to a bowl. Add brown sugar, almonds and lemon zest.

3 Peel pears and apples, cut into quarters, remove cores and slice finely. Gently toss fruit in a bowl with lemon juice, ginger and caster sugar. Divide fruit between ramekins, pressing it in (it will reduce down during cooking).

4 Spoon crumble over fruit, mounding it in the middle of each dish so a little steam can escape around the sides. Bake for about 30 minutes, or until juices are bubbling through and crumble topping is golden. If crumble top browns before fruit is done, drape a piece of tin foil over the top of the crumble, lower the temperature and keep cooking until fruit is ready. Serve hottish or at room temperature.

apple and blackberry pie

ready in 1 hour 10 minutes, plus chilling | serves 8

This is a good-looking pie, full of fruit and rich juices. Adding a pinch of cinnamon to blackberries really enhances their luscious, sweet earthy warmth.

1 Preheat oven to 190°C (regular bake).

2 Sift flour with salt. Put flour and butter in the bowl of a food processor fitted with the chopping blade. Process briefly until mixture resembles coarse breadcrumbs. Mix egg and water together and pour into the processor through the feed tube. Pulse together until the mixture gathers in large clumps. Tip dough onto a dry, lightly floured surface and knead until smooth. Wrap in plastic food wrap and chill until firm.

3 Peel and core apples, slice and put them in a bowl. Mix lemon juice through, and add blackberries, cinnamon, sugar and cornflour. Toss gently.

4 Cut off a little more than a third of the dough for the top of the pie. Roll out the rest of the dough on a lightly floured surface and line into a 24cm enamel pie plate. Trim off excess pastry. Spoon apples and blackberries into pie, mounding them towards the centre.

5 Roll out remaining pastry to a 30cm round on a lightly floured surface and place on top of pie. Trim off excess pastry and crimp edges together. Make a steam hole in the centre of the pie, then brush pie with beaten egg white and sprinkle with caster sugar. Have a baking sheet heating in the bottom third of the oven. Put pie plate on baking sheet and cook for 35–40 minutes, or until pastry is a good golden brown and fruit is tender (if the pastry colours too quickly, drape it with tin foil to deflect the heat). Serve hot with ice cream, or cold with cream or homemade custard.

350g standard flour
pinch of salt
150g unsalted cold butter, firm but pliable, cubed
1 medium (size 6) free-range egg, lightly beaten
100ml chilled water
600g (about 3 large) Granny Smith or cooking apples
1 Tbsp lemon juice
250g frozen or fresh blackberries
¼ tsp ground cinnamon
100g caster sugar, plus extra for sprinkling on top
2 Tbsp cornflour
1 egg white, lightly beaten
ice cream, cream or homemade custard (page 97), for serving

apple brown betty

ready in 55 minutes | serves 6

This American no-fuss family favourite is made with fruit (usually apple), layered with bread in the form of crumbs, cubes or, in this case, small triangles, and some sort of sweetening. This version uses golden syrup, which gives the bread topping a lovely crisp finish; lemon zest and juice keep the sweetness from overpowering the dish.

8 slices white bread, toast thickness
60g unsalted butter, softened
600g (about 3 large) Granny Smith or other tart
   apples
125ml golden syrup
finely grated zest and juice of 1 lemon
homemade custard (page 97) or vanilla ice cream,
   to serve

1 Preheat oven to 200°C (regular bake). Make the dessert in a deep enamel pudding dish about 20cm x 14cm wide and 5cm deep (or something similar).

2 Spread bread generously with soft butter, then remove the crusts and cut each slice into triangles.

3 Peel, core and finely slice the apples. Make three layers of buttered bread and two layers of apple: drizzle each layer with golden syrup, scatter with a little lemon zest and moisten with lemon juice. Allow plenty of bread triangles and about two-thirds of the golden syrup for the top. Put this last layer of bread buttered side up. Cover loosely with a sheet of baking paper, then with tin foil (the tin foil will stick without the baking paper).

4 Bake for 15 minutes, remove foil and baking paper and continue cooking for a further 15–25 minutes, until apples are tender and the bread topping is golden and crusty. Serve hottish with custard or ice cream.

queen of puddings

ready in 1 hour | serves 4

The origin of this traditional British pudding dates back to the 17th century, but it's unclear which queen it was named after. Never mind. It is, quite simply, one of the best homely inexpensive puddings.

100g fresh white breadcrumbs (4–5 slices white bread,
   toast thickness)
finely grated zest of 1 lemon
100g caster sugar
400ml whole milk
45g unsalted butter
2 medium (size 6) free-range eggs, at room
   temperature, separated
4 Tbsp strawberry or plum jam or conserve
extra caster sugar, for dredging

1 Preheat oven to 170°C (regular bake). Lightly butter four deep ramekins and set them on a baking sheet.

2 In a bowl, mix breadcrumbs, lemon zest and 1 tablespoon of the sugar. Heat milk and butter in a saucepan until butter has just melted, then pour over crumbs. Stir well. Leave to soak for 15 minutes, then stir in egg yolks.

3 Pour custard into ramekins. Bake for about 20 minutes, until custards are just set and have browned slightly around the edges. Remove from oven and spoon the jam or conserve on top of them.

4 Whisk egg whites in a grease-free bowl until they form stiff peaks. Gradually whisk in the remaining sugar, and continue whisking until stiff and glossy. Spoon on top of the custards – you'll probably only need two-thirds of the meringue. Dredge (dust) with a little caster sugar. Return custards to oven and bake for about 10 minutes, until meringue is crisp and lightly golden. Serve warm or at room temperature.

apple sponge with custard

ready in 1 hour 5 minutes | serves 8 or more

This makes a large pudding, but it is so good the next day for breakfast or morning tea (it reheats well in the microwave) that I've deliberately made a generous amount. It's also surprisingly light to eat, so you may find everyone has seconds! Instead of making one large pudding, you could make it in individual ovenproof dishes.

1.2kg (about 6 large) Granny Smith
   or cooking apples
70g caster sugar
finely grated zest and juice of 1
   large lemon
2 Tbsp water
200g unsalted butter, cubed and
   softened
170g caster sugar
3 medium (size 6) free-range eggs,
   at room temperature
270g self-raising flour
150ml milk, at room temperature
icing sugar, for dusting (optional)
homemade custard (page 97),
   to serve

1 Preheat oven to 180°C (regular bake). Butter a Pyrex dish 33cm × 23cm × 5cm.

2 Peel apples, cut into quarters, remove cores and slice thinly. Put apples in a large bowl with the first measure of sugar, the lemon zest and juice. Stir in water, then tip into buttered dish.

3 Put butter in a bowl and beat with an electric beater until creamy and loose. Beat in second measure of caster sugar a tablespoon at a time and continue beating until fluffy and lighter in colour (creamed; see cooking class on page 111). Beat eggs together with a fork, then add them gradually to the creamed butter and sugar, adding 1–2 tablespoons of the measured flour about halfway through beating to help stabilise the mixture. Sift over one-third of the remaining flour and fold it in with one-third of the milk. Repeat twice more with remaining flour and milk.

4 Spread sponge mixture over apples. Bake for about 40 minutes, or until apples are tender and bubbling, and the sponge is golden, firm and crusty around the edges. Serve hot or warm, dusted with icing sugar if you like, with a jug of homemade custard.

caramelised banana wraps

ready in 10 minutes | serves 4

These wraps are unbelievably scrumptious. With chocolate and hazelnuts, caramelised bananas and ice cream, how could they be anything else?

4 ripe but firm bananas
2 Tbsp unsalted butter
100g demerara sugar
4 soft flour tortillas
250g ready-made chocolate hazelnut spread (e.g. Nutella)
200–250g vanilla ice cream (a small tub is more than enough)
cocoa powder, for dusting

1 Peel bananas and slice each on the diagonal into 4–5 pieces. Heat a large non-stick frying pan over a medium heat and drop in the butter. Coat banana slices with sugar and add to pan once butter is sizzling. Cook until golden, then turn pieces carefully using two spoons and continue cooking until golden. Transfer to a plate. (To clean pan, let it cool, fill with water and soak for 10 minutes – the sugar will then easily lift off.)

2 Warm tortillas either wrapped in paper towels in a microwave, or wrapped in tin foil in an oven. Spread generously with chocolate hazelnut spread, put banana slices in the centre of each tortilla, then add small scoops of ice cream. Roll up. Slice on the diagonal and arrange on plates. Dust with cocoa powder and serve immediately.

homemade custard

ready in 20 minutes | serves 6

If you prefer a smooth finish, strain the cooked custard to catch the tiny dots of vanilla seeds (I leave them in because I like the extra flavour). To prevent a skin forming on the top of the cooked custard, sprinkle with a little caster sugar and cover with a lid or plate. Just give the custard a quick stir before serving, and transfer it to a serving jug or bowl.

300ml whole milk
½ vanilla pod
3 medium (size 6) free-range egg yolks, at room temperature
1 level tsp arrowroot
2 Tbsp caster sugar
extra caster sugar, for sprinkling (optional)

1 Put milk in a small saucepan. Scrape in seeds from vanilla pod and add the pod too. Heat gently until warm (not hot), then remove from heat and leave to infuse for 10 minutes.

2 Beat egg yolks, arrowroot and sugar together in a small bowl with a wooden spoon for 2–3 minutes until creamy and smooth. Blend in the milk. Wipe out saucepan, then return mixture to pan over a low to medium heat. Stir constantly with a wooden spoon until custard thickens and coats the back of the spoon (see cooking class on page 84). On no account let it reach boiling point, or it will curdle.

3 Remove vanilla pod (the vanilla pod can be washed, dried and reused), then pour custard into a bowl and serve hot, or sprinkle with caster sugar, cool then cover and refrigerate.

pear and maple pudding

ready in 35 minutes, plus 1 hour 30 minutes steaming | serves 8

Golden and warming, this old-fashioned steamed pudding is bound to brighten gloomy wintry days. Use genuine maple syrup, not a sugary substitute. To steam the pudding, choose a saucepan that the basin fits into with enough room for steam to circulate, and with a tight-fitting lid. Check the water level in the pan about halfway through cooking. If water is low, top it up with boiling water from a kettle.

butter for greasing pudding basin and paper covering

3 level Tbsp maple syrup

1 large, firm pear

150g unsalted butter, softened

150g caster sugar

2 medium (size 6) free-range eggs, at room temperature

150g self-raising flour

finely grated zest of 1 lemon

5 Tbsp milk, at room temperature

cream or ice cream and extra maple syrup, to serve

1 Generously grease a 4-cup (1-litre) china pudding basin with butter. Prepare a paper covering as described on page 110.

2 Put maple syrup in bottom of basin. Peel the pear, cut into quarters, remove core, and slice. Arrange sliced pear in bottom of basin.

3 In a bowl, beat butter with an electric beater until creamy and loose, then beat in caster sugar a tablespoon at a time and continue beating until fluffy and lighter in colour (creamed; see cooking class on page 111). You'll need to stop the machine and scrape the sides of the bowl down several times. Beat eggs together with a fork, then add them gradually to creamed butter and sugar, adding 1–2 tablespoons of the measured flour halfway through beating to help stabilise the mixture. Sift flour over and fold in with lemon zest, adding milk as you do so. Turn mixture into buttered basin. Cover with buttered paper and tie securely with string.

4 Transfer pudding to a large, deep (rather than wide) saucepan with a trivet, or put a small clean cloth under the pudding basin to stop it clattering during cooking. Fill the pan with hot water to come about one-third of the way up the pudding basin. Cover pan with a tight-fitting lid. Bring water to the boil (you'll see the steam), then turn the heat to the lowest setting and gently steam pudding for 1½ hours. Top up with boiling water from a kettle if water runs low.

5 Remove pudding basin from pan, then snip the string off and remove paper. Cover pudding with a serving plate, invert and leave for 10 minutes to ensure it drops perfectly, then remove basin. Serve with extra maple syrup and runny cream or vanilla ice cream.

steamed date pudding

ready in 30 minutes, plus 1 hour 30 minutes steaming | serves 8 or more

This is a really easy, light and very moreish sponge pud – just perfect for wintry days.

butter for greasing pudding basin
    and paper covering

120g self-raising flour

pinch of salt

½ tsp mixed spice

90g unsalted butter, at room
    temperature, roughly chopped

30g fresh white breadcrumbs

3 Tbsp soft brown sugar

170g fresh dates, pitted and
    chopped

finely grated zest of 1 lemon

2 medium (size 6) free-range eggs,
    at room temperature

1 Tbsp golden syrup

2 Tbsp milk, at room temperature

homemade custard (page 97),
    to serve

1 Grease a 5-cup (1.25-litre) china pudding basin with butter. Prepare a paper covering as described on page 110.

2 Sift flour, salt and mixed spice into a bowl. Rub in butter with two round-bladed knives or a pastry blender, and stir in breadcrumbs, sugar, dates and lemon zest.

3 Whisk eggs with golden syrup and milk, then tip into the dry ingredients. Mix with a wooden spoon until smooth.

4 Turn mixture into buttered basin, then cover with buttered paper and tie securely with string. Transfer pudding to a large, deep (rather than wide) saucepan with a trivet or put a small clean cloth under the pudding basin to stop it clattering during cooking. Fill pan with hot water to come about one-third of the way up the basin, and cover with a tight-fitting lid. Bring water to the boil, then turn heat to lowest setting and gently steam pudding for 1½ hours. Top up with boiling water from a kettle if water runs low.

5 When ready, remove pudding basin from pan, snip off string and remove paper. Cover pudding basin with a serving plate, invert and leave for 10 minutes to drop, then remove basin. Serve pudding with hot custard.

apricot upside-down gingerbread

ready in 1 hour 25 minutes | serves 8 or more

Sticky, gooey, soft, moist and tangy – this cake has got the lot! Serve warm with whipped or runny cream, homemade custard or vanilla ice cream.

topping
170g dried apricots
250ml water
peel of ½ lemon
75g butter
120g soft brown sugar

gingerbread
120g butter
180g black treacle
120g caster sugar
300g standard flour
1 level tsp baking soda
½ tsp salt
1 tsp ground ginger
1 tsp ground cinnamon
1 medium (size 6) free-range egg,
   lightly beaten
220ml buttermilk

to serve
whipped or runny cream,
   homemade custard (page 97) or
   vanilla ice cream

1 Preheat oven to 180°C (regular bake). Line the base and sides of a 22cm cake tin with baking paper.

2 Make the topping first. Put apricots in a small saucepan with water and lemon peel. Bring to the boil and cook gently for about 10 minutes, or until tender. Strain, discarding the lemon peel.

3 Melt butter and brown sugar together; warm gently but don't let it get too hot. Pour into prepared tin and lay apricots on top.

4 To make the cake, warm butter, treacle and sugar in a small saucepan until butter is melted and sugar is dissolved (don't boil). Cool for several minutes. Sift together flour, soda, salt and spices into a large bowl. Make a well in the centre, then add beaten egg and buttermilk and the cooled syrup mixture. Beat just until smooth. Pour on top of apricots in tin.

5 Bake cake for about 45 minutes, or until it springs back to the touch and a skewer inserted into the centre comes out clean. Cool in the tin for 12–15 minutes, then turn out onto a warmed cake plate. Serve warm with whipped or runny cream, homemade custard or vanilla ice cream.

winter crumble

ready in 1 hour 10 minutes | makes 6

The best sort of crumble is one with tender fruit, juices bubbling up around the edge, fruit with a slight tang or bite to it, and a tender crumble crust, not too buttery or powdery, maybe with crunchy nuts. Choose ripe, but not squishy, tamarillos for this crumble. Firm ones are hard to peel and don't ooze appealing crimson juices as they cook. A scoop of good-quality vanilla ice cream is great with this – have a few bites of crumble, then drop a scoop of ice cream into the bowl.

crumble

75g standard flour
120g butter, cubed
½ tsp ground cinnamon
100g toasted, skinned and roughly chopped hazelnuts (see page 127)
100g rolled oats
3 Tbsp soft brown sugar

fruit

8 ripe but firm tamarillos
600g (about 3 large) Granny Smith or other tart apples
5 Tbsp soft brown sugar
finely grated zest of 1 lemon

1 Preheat oven to 180°C (regular bake). Lightly butter six ovenproof ramekins and put them in a shallow ovenproof dish in case juices bubble over during cooking.

2 To make the crumble, blend flour and butter together in a food processor until mixture resembles coarse breadcrumbs. Alternatively, cut butter into flour using two knives or a pastry blender. Transfer to a clean bowl. Add cinnamon, hazelnuts, rolled oats and brown sugar.

3 Plunge tamarillos into a saucepan of boiling water, count to 30, then use a slotted spoon to transfer them to a bowl of cold water. Peel and slice thickly (if the peel won't come off easily, return tamarillos to hot water for a few more seconds).

4 Peel, quarter and core apples, then slice finely. Put apple in a bowl with tamarillos and add brown sugar and lemon zest. Divide fruit between ramekins. Spoon crumble on top, mounding it nice and high as the fruit will sink as it cooks.

5 Bake the crumbles in the dish for about 30 minutes, or until juices are bubbling through and crumble topping is golden. If crumble top browns before fruit is done, drape a piece of tin foil over the top of the ramekins, lower the temperature and keep cooking until fruit is ready.

creamy rice pudding

ready in 35 minutes | serves 4–6

Orange rind, cinnamon, vanilla and orange blossom water give this creamy rice pudding an exotic perfume and flavour. Keep the heat low, and whip in enough cream at the end to give it a rich creamy texture.

250g medium-grain rice (I use Australian medium-grain calrose rice)

small piece cinnamon stick

small piece vanilla pod, split

3 strips orange rind

1 litre milk

6 Tbsp caster sugar

75ml cream

1 Tbsp orange blossom water

slivered oranges, ground cinnamon, sugar or vanilla sugar and vanilla pods, to garnish (optional)

1 Put the rice in a saucepan, cover with cold water and bring to the boil, stirring often. Drain.

2 Return rice to a clean saucepan and add the cinnamon stick, vanilla pod, orange rind and milk. Bring to a gentle boil, then immediately turn the heat down and simmer very gently for about 20 minutes, or until the rice is tender, stirring often; the pudding should be wonderfully creamy.

3 Remove the cinnamon stick and vanilla pod and blend in the sugar, cream and orange blossom water. Spoon into bowls and serve warmish.

4 If you like, top with a piece of vanilla pod and slivered oranges dusted with ground cinnamon and sprinkled with sugar – this can then be glazed under the grill until the sugar caramelises.

sticky apricot pudding

ready in 25 minutes, plus 3 hours steaming | serves 8 or more

This is the pudding of all puddings. Should you be starving, craving sweetness and longing for a bit of old-fashioned pud, this is the one.

1 Grease a 4-cup (1-litre) china pudding basin with butter. Prepare a paper covering as described on page 110.

2 Sift flour, salt and baking powder together into a bowl. Add butter and cut it through the flour with two knives until mixture resembles coarse breadcrumbs. Mix in chopped apricots and sultanas, then the milk and egg.

3 Put one-third of the honey in the bottom of the basin, then spoon in half the pudding mixture. Put in a second third of the honey and the last of the pudding, then top with the rest of the honey.

4 Cover with buttered paper and tie securely with string. Transfer pudding to a large, deep (rather than wide) saucepan with a trivet or put a small clean cloth under the pudding basin to stop it clattering during cooking. Fill the pan with hot water to come about one-third of the way up the pudding basin. Cover pan with a tight-fitting lid. Bring the water to the boil (you'll see the steam), then turn the heat to the lowest setting and gently steam pudding for 3 hours. Top up with boiling water from a kettle when the water runs low.

5 When ready, remove pudding basin from pan, snip off string and remove paper. Cover pudding basin with a serving plate, invert, then leave pudding for 10 minutes to drop.

6 Remove the bowl. The honey and apricots make this pudding a little stickier than most steamed puddings, but any little bits stuck to the bowl can be removed and put back in place on the pudding. Serve hottish with ice cream, cream or homemade custard.

butter for greasing pudding basin
   and paper covering
175g standard flour
pinch of salt
1½ tsp baking powder
100g unsalted butter, cubed
125g dried apricots, chopped
120g golden sultanas
250ml milk, at room temperature
1 medium (size 6) free-range egg
200ml liquid honey
vanilla ice cream, cream or
   homemade custard (page 97),
   to serve

A cooking class with Julie

Steaming

Steamed puddings are a classic English dessert. They can be made with suet – the fat surrounding the kidneys or found on the loins of beef and mutton – or with butter. In this book they are made with butter and are based on the rubbing-in method (see cooking class on page 82) or the creaming method (see cooking class on page 111).

The puddings are cooked in a thick china bowl which offers some protection from the heat, ensuring gentle cooking. Many cooks use heatproof glass (such as Pyrex) or aluminium pudding basins to good effect, but a china bowl has the advantage of holding the heat longer than glass or aluminium, and keeps the pudding warmer for longer once it is cooked.

Covering the pudding with baking paper prevents the steam from making it soggy, and putting a pleat in the paper will give the pudding room to expand. A string handle makes it easy to remove the hot pudding from the saucepan of steaming water. Here's how to do it: take a large piece of baking paper, fold it in half so you have a double thickness, and make a pleat on the fold (picture 1). Open pleat and grease paper with butter to prevent it sticking (picture 2). Refold pleat (picture 3), then position paper buttered side down on the pudding basin. Cut a piece of string

1

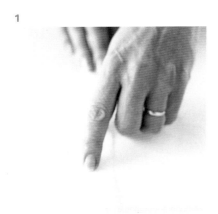

2

3

4

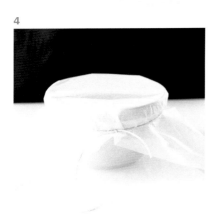

5

6

7

long enough to loop around the basin twice and to also to form a handle. Tie a double thickness of string around the rim to hold the paper in place. Bring string over the top of the basin and loop it through the string around the rim, then take it back again and tie in a knot to form the handle (pictures 4 to 6).

Choose a saucepan which the basin fits into with enough room for steam to circulate (picture 7), and that has a tight-fitting lid. To stop the bowl clattering as the pudding cooks, put a small clean cloth under the pudding basin. Fill the pan with hot water to come about one-third of the way up the pudding basin. Cover pan with lid. Bring water to the boil (you'll see the steam), then turn the heat to the lowest setting and gently steam pudding as directed in the recipe.

Check the water level in the pan about halfway through cooking. If water is low, top it up with boiling water from a kettle – not hot tap water as that will slow the boiling and cooking. Lift off the lid and immediately flip it over and pour off any water accumulated on the inside of the lid. If you raise the lid above the pudding and let this water drip down onto it, it will make the top of the pudding soggy. Pour water around the sides of the pudding basin, replace the lid and carry on steaming the pudding until the cooking time is up.

Remove pudding basin from the pan, lifting it up with the string handle, snip off the string and remove the paper. Cover basin with a warmed serving plate and invert, then leave for 10 minutes to ensure that the pudding has dropped. Serve puddings hot, cut into slices. Leftover steamed puddings can be reheated in a microwave or between two plates over a pan of simmering water; or, for a decadent treat, sliced and sugared and lightly fried in butter.

Using the creaming method

In this method butter and sugar are whipped together until they are like a thick, fluffy cream, eggs are beaten in, then the dry ingredients are folded in. The top of the cooked cake is slightly moist, and can be a little sticky. It's generally smooth and flat; although small cakes, such as cupcakes, are often raised. The crumb is even-textured, soft and tender. The method makes a richer cake than the whisking method does. It is used for classic cakes such as Victoria sandwich (a split cake sandwiched together with jam, named after Queen Victoria). Butter improves the keeping quality of cakes made with the creaming method; the higher the proportion of butter in the recipe, the longer the cake will keep. Most will keep well for 2–3 days in a cake tin.

The creaming method causes cooks more problems than any other cake-making methods, but with a little knowledge success can be achieved.

It is essential that the butter be at room temperature (18–20°C), as cold butter cannot be creamed sufficiently, and that the other ingredients are also at room temperature to ensure that air can be trapped during mixing. On a cold day, the butter can be gently microwaved in bursts of 5–10 seconds on high until it is pliable. Alternatively, the butter can be put in a bowl and the bowl put somewhere warm for a few minutes, but the butter *must not melt*. Melted butter will not cream properly because it cannot hold air, and it will make the cake heavy.

1

The best bowl to use is a deepish mixing bowl which is wider at the top than at the bottom (picture 1). This confines the ingredients to be creamed, making it faster to cream them, and the wide top allows room to fold in the dry ingredients. In a wide-bottomed bowl you end up chasing the ingredients around the bowl (if using a hand-held electric beater, for instance, the beaters flick the mixture to one side of the

2   3

bowl; you move the beater there only to find that once it gathers up the mixture it flicks it to another side of the bowl).

Beat the butter to loosen it first, then gradually beat in the caster sugar (picture 2), and continue beating until the butter and sugar are paler in colour, thick and fluffy, and nicely soft (picture 3). Thorough beating is required to break down the sugar crystals and produce a light, fine-textured cake. Failure to do this sufficiently is the main cause of curdling (the mixture separating) once eggs are added. Make sure all the sugar is mixed in, because if any crystals are left around the sides of the mixture they will cause speckling on top of the cake. Use caster sugar, not granulated, because it will break down more readily.

Use fresh eggs, because egg white thins down as the egg ages and the wateriness of older eggs can be difficult for the fat and sugar to absorb. Have the eggs at room temperature, like the butter and sugar, to help the ingredients mix together. If the eggs are taken straight from the refrigerator, immerse them in a bowl of hottish water for a few minutes, then leave them at room temperature for 10 minutes before proceeding with the recipe. Alternatively, break the eggs into a warmed china bowl, beat lightly, then leave bowl immersed in warm water for 5–10 minutes. If using only egg yolks, ensure the chalazae (cord of the egg) are nipped off with a piece of eggshell, and that they go with the egg whites, not the yolks.

4

Beat eggs together with a fork to break them up, then gradually beat them into the creamed butter and sugar (picture 4). If the eggs are added too fast, and without thorough beating between additions, the mixture can separate. If the added weight of butter and sugar in the recipe is over 225g, the eggs may be added whole, one at a time, beating well after adding each egg. Adding a small amount of the flour while beating in the eggs – generally, 1 tablespoon per egg – will help stabilise the creamed mixture and prevent curdling.

If the mixture curdles due to cold ingredients, all may not be lost. Stand the bowl in a sink of warm water and beat vigorously – you may rescue it. If despite your hard work the mixture stays curdled, carry on with the recipe because it would be wasteful to throw out butter, sugar and eggs. The cake will not be as light and the texture will be denser, but it will still be perfectly edible and hopefully you will have learnt some lessons to help towards success next time.

The next step is to add the dry ingredients, and any liquid called for, without deflating the mixture. Sift flour with a pinch of salt to aerate it, then sift it over the top of the

5

6

7

8

creamed mixture. Use a large metal spoon to fold in flour along with any other dry ingredients (picture 5). A wooden spoon is not as effective as a large metal spoon, as it doesn't scoop the mixture off the sides of the bowl as cleanly as the metal spoon. Do not beat, as beating will make the cake tough. Any milk or liquid called for in the recipe should also be at room temperature to prevent curdling. As a precaution, when adding liquids or fats such as sour cream, add the flour in three lots, and the milk, liquids or fats in two or three lots, one after each addition of flour (picture 6). This helps gently combine everything. The cake will not find its own level during baking, so pile it into the lined tin and spread with a knife until smooth (pictures 7 and 8).

When a creamed cake is cooked, it should be an even golden colour, and should spring back when gently pressed with the finger. It should also be shrinking slightly from the sides of the cake tin. It can be checked in the centre using a fine skewer – but use a bamboo skewer, not a shiny metal one, because uncooked mixture simply slips off metal but will cling to bamboo. The skewer should come out clean.

Cool cake in tin very briefly, to avoid it sweating (unless directed otherwise – generally when there is a heavy fruit component which could cause the cake to split if it is turned out while still hot). Then go round between the cake and the tin with a flat-bladed knife to loosen the cake from the tin. Invert onto a cooling rack lined with a piece of baking paper and peel off the paper from the bottom of the cake (picture 9)

9

10

if it is still attached – sometimes it remains in the tin. If directed, cover cake with a second cooling rack also lined with baking paper (or use a plate) and flip cake back over top uppermost, then lift off cooling rack or plate (this depends on whether the bottom of the cake is to be presented as the top – desirable when a flat, smooth surface is required for icing). Cool cake away from draughts (picture 10). Pictures 9 and 10 show limoncello sponge (page 16), made with sour cream.

chocolate

chocolate fudge pots

ready in 40 minutes, plus cooling | serves 6

These fudge pots can be made several hours ahead, but keep them at room temperature, not in the refrigerator. Serve cream in a jug and encourage everyone to pour cream into the centre of the puddings.

1 Preheat oven to 180°C (regular bake). Lightly butter six ramekins with a 200ml capacity. Cut six long strips of baking paper to go around the outside of the ramekins to support the mixture as it bakes, and tie this on with string. The paper should come about 3cm above the top of the ramekin.

2 Gently melt butter in a heavy saucepan, add chocolate and stir until melted and smooth.

3 Separate eggs, putting egg whites in a grease-free bowl and yolks in a large bowl. Mix caster sugar, brown sugar and egg yolks together. Blend in chocolate and butter mixture, then stir in flour and ground almonds.

4 Whip egg whites with an electric beater until stiff but not dry, sprinkle in cream of tartar and beat for 1 minute more. Mix a large spoonful of egg white into the chocolate mixture to loosen it, then using a large spoon carefully fold in the rest; don't beat.

5 Spoon mixture into prepared ramekins, filling them right to the top of the ramekin. Transfer ramekins to a baking sheet. Bake for about 20 minutes. The tops should be cracking, but the centres should still have plenty of wobble. Cool to room temperature before serving. To serve, remove paper and dust tops with icing sugar.

250g unsalted butter, plus extra
  for greasing ramekins
250g good-quality dark chocolate
  with at least 70% cocoa solids,
  broken into squares or roughly
  chopped
6 medium (size 6) free-range eggs,
  at room temperature
160g caster sugar
35g (about 3 Tbsp) light brown
  sugar
35g standard flour
3 Tbsp ground almonds
½ tsp cream of tartar
icing sugar, for sprinkling
250ml cream, to serve

quick tiramisu

ready in 15 minutes | serves 4–6

The literal translation of tiramisu is 'pick me up', which a shot of good espresso coffee invariably does. This is a quick but nonetheless delicious version of this popular dessert.

125g sponge fingers (also known as boudoir biscuits or lady finger biscuits)

125ml espresso coffee, sweetened

3 Tbsp coffee liqueur, such as Tia Maria

200ml cream

seeds scraped from ¼ vanilla pod

200ml homemade custard (page 97) or ready-made custard

1 Tbsp cocoa powder sifted with 1 Tbsp caster sugar

1 Cut sponge fingers to fit chosen glasses (split the biscuits in half lengthways for long glasses, or cut them in half around the waist for shorter ones, or into quarters for ice cream dishes). Put biscuits in a shallow dish. Mix coffee and coffee liqueur and spoon over biscuits. If serving the dessert in tall glasses, line the glasses with coffee-soaked biscuits.

2 Lightly whip the cream with the vanilla seeds. Assemble dessert with layers of whipped cream, custard and coffee-soaked biscuits. Dust the top with cocoa and caster sugar, and refrigerate desserts until ready to serve.

devil's chocolate cake

ready in 50 minutes, plus cooling | serves 8 or more

This cake is easily made using the warming method (see cooking class on page 165), which is perfect for cooks who don't have a machine to whip or cream ingredients. It's a good-flavoured cake with a fine soft crumb, and the sour cream chocolate topping is a handy one to add to your repertoire.

110g unsalted butter

100g good-quality dark chocolate with at least 60% cocoa solids, broken into squares or chopped

100g muscovado sugar

1 Tbsp golden syrup

160g standard flour

pinch of salt

4 level Tbsp cocoa powder

½ tsp baking soda

2 large (size 7) free-range eggs, at room temperature, beaten lightly

½ tsp vanilla extract

100ml milk, at room temperature

topping

200g good-quality dark chocolate with at least 60% cocoa solids, broken into squares or chopped

200g sour cream

1 Preheat oven to 170°C (regular bake). Grease a 21cm diameter × 5cm deep cake tin and line the base with baking paper.

2 Put butter, chocolate, sugar and golden syrup in a large bowl and set it over a small saucepan of simmering water. Stir until chocolate and butter have melted, then remove bowl from pan and let the contents cool.

3 Sift flour, salt, cocoa powder and baking soda onto a piece of paper, then sift them again into a large bowl. Make a well in the centre and drop in the eggs, then add the melted chocolate mixture along with the vanilla extract. Carefully stir together with a large spoon, adding the milk in small amounts as the batter stiffens; don't beat.

4 Spoon mixture into prepared cake tin. Bake for 25 minutes, or until slightly shrinking from sides of tin and springy to the touch. Cool in the tin, then turn onto a plate lined with baking paper, peel paper off bottom of cake, cover cake with a cooling rack, flip and remove paper and plate.

5 To make the topping, melt chocolate in a large bowl set over a saucepan of just-simmering water. Let chocolate cool to room temperature, then blend in the sour cream. Spread over top and sides of cake. To serve, cut into wedges with a serrated knife.

upside-down chocolate amaretti cheesecakes

ready in 1 hour 10 minutes, plus cooling | serves 6

These rich and curiously bitter-sweet cheesecakes make a fitting end to a lavish meal, especially good when served with espresso coffee. They can be kept in a cool place, but not refrigerated, for up to 8 hours before serving.

cheesecakes

200g good-quality dark chocolate with at least 60% cocoa solids, broken into squares or roughly chopped

400g cream cheese

150g sour cream

60g caster sugar

2 Tbsp standard flour

3 medium (size 6) free-range eggs, at room temperature

base

100g amaretti biscuits (almond-flavoured macaroons)

60g unsalted butter, melted

topping

4–6 amaretti biscuits, crushed

50g good-quality dark chocolate with at least 60% cocoa solids, melted

1 Preheat oven to 160°C (regular bake). Choose six ramekins with a 200ml capacity and put a disc of baking paper in the bottom of each.

2 To make the cheesecakes, melt chocolate in a heatproof bowl over a small saucepan of simmering water. Remove from heat and cool.

3 Crush biscuits for the base (easily done by putting biscuits in a large sealable bag and crushing with a rolling pin). Transfer biscuits to a bowl and blend in the butter. Press mixture into the bottoms of the ramekins. Chill.

4 Put cream cheese, sour cream, caster sugar and flour in a large bowl and beat with an electric beater until smooth. Break the eggs into a small bowl, beat with a fork, then beat into the cream cheese mixture a little at a time. Fold in melted chocolate.

5 Spoon mixture into ramekins. Put ramekins on a baking sheet and bake for about 50 minutes. The cheesecakes will puff up, crack a little and look like they'll topple over, but they won't. As they cool they'll sink a little and nestle back into the ramekins. This is all normal behaviour. Cool them in the oven with the door ajar. Invert onto plates to serve, first running a flat-bladed knife around the inside of the ramekins, then peel off paper if attached. If they are difficult to turn out, dip briefly in a sink of hot water first.

6 Before serving, crumble over broken amaretti. Dip fork in melted chocolate and drizzle over the top of desserts. Serve immediately.

peach and chocolate tart

ready in 1 hour 15 minutes | serves 8

If peach stones are difficult to extract, cut them out with a serrated grapefruit knife (see page 43). Cut off any flesh adhering to the stones, chop finely and add to the amaretti mixture. The tart can be prepared up to 3 hours before serving, providing the fruit is well drained before arranging in the pastry case so it doesn't make the pastry soggy. This tart also works well with nectarines.

1 Preheat oven to 180°C (fanbake).

2 Roll out pastry on a lightly floured surface and line into a 21cm loose-bottomed flan ring set on a baking sheet. Prick pastry base with a fork, then refrigerate until firm. To bake blind (see cooking class on page 83), line pastry with light tin foil or crumpled tissue paper and fill with baking beans. Cook for 20 minutes until golden around the edges and browned on the bottom. Remove foil or paper and baking beans, then brush the inside of the pastry with egg yolk and return to oven for a further 5 minutes.

3 Meanwhile, put lemon juice in a large bowl. Peel peaches, then cut them into thin slices, discarding the stones, and drop slices into the bowl as they are prepared. Gently toss the peach slices in the lemon juice, then cover until required (the peaches can be prepared up to 30 minutes before assembling the tart). If using nectarines, wash and dry but don't peel them, and prepare as described above.

4 Tip peaches or nectarines onto a double thickness of paper towels and pat them dry. Arrange fruit slices on top of pastry. Put crushed amaretti biscuits in a bowl with caster sugar. Sift the cocoa powder over. Spoon topping over the fruit and dot with butter. Lower oven heat to 170°C and bake for 15–20 minutes, or until the top is browned and the fruit is tender. Serve hottish or warm.

400g ready-made sweet shortcrust or buttercrust pastry
1 medium (size 6) free-range egg yolk
2 Tbsp lemon juice
800–900g fresh, firmish peaches
120g amaretti biscuits, coarsely crushed
50g caster sugar
4 Tbsp cocoa powder
1 Tbsp butter

brown sugar meringue with chocolate cream

ready in 1 hour 20 minutes, plus cooling and chilling | serves 8 or more

This gâteau is sweet and a bit chewy with a hint of caramel bitterness. Use good-quality dark chocolate with a high percentage of cocoa solids.

meringue
160g soft brown sugar
4 medium (size 6) free-range egg whites

filling
100g good-quality dark chocolate with at least 70% cocoa solids, broken into squares or roughly chopped
3 Tbsp water
200ml cream

to finish
icing sugar, for dusting

1 Preheat oven to 140°C (regular bake). Put two 20cm flan rings (without bases) on baking sheets lined with baking paper. Line inside of rings with strips of baking paper (use a dab of meringue later on to hold the strips of paper in place), or lightly brush inside of rings with melted butter and dust with flour.

2 Push brown sugar through a coarse sieve. Whisk egg whites until soft peaks form, then gradually beat in the brown sugar 1 tablespoon at a time. Continue whisking for 2–3 minutes until thick and satiny (see cooking class on page 134). Divide meringue between the flan rings, being careful not to knock out air. Smooth the surface with a knife.

3 Bake for 1 hour – preferably on the same shelf, otherwise alternate the positions of the meringues once or twice during baking. Remove from oven and cool for 10 minutes. Carefully slip a slim, sharp knife between meringue and flan ring to loosen, then leave to cool completely.

4 When cool, put a light cooling rack on top of each meringue round (one at a time), invert, loosen from flan ring, remove ring and any paper attached to the meringue, then turn meringue topside up again.

5 Melt chocolate with water in a microwave (try 30 seconds, stir, then 20 seconds, stir, then 10 seconds), or in a small saucepan over a gentle heat, stirring often. Cool. Whip cream until just thick and holding shape – and this is important – if it is too stiff, it will turn buttery by the time the chocolate is folded in (if this happens, add a little liquid cream; it may help). Pour in chocolate and gently fold cream and chocolate together with a large spoon.

6 Put one meringue round on a cake stand or plate, then spread with chocolate cream filling. Put the other meringue round on top and dust with icing sugar. Refrigerate for at least 1 hour before serving, or up to 8 hours (it keeps well, refrigerated, for 2–3 days).

hazelnut and chocolate tart

ready in 1 hour 5 minutes, plus cooling | serves 12 – you only need a sliver!

This dessert is a killer! Drop-dead gorgeous, even when it is made with ready-made pastry. Leftovers will keep well for a day or two. If your oven doesn't cook the bottom of pastry very well, blind-bake the pastry case before filling. To do this (see cooking class on page 83), line pastry with tin foil, fill with baking beans and bake for 12 minutes, then remove from oven and cool for 10 minutes before filling and returning to the oven. Once pastry is a good golden colour, you can protect it and the top of the tart by draping it loosely with tin foil.

1 Preheat oven to 180°C (regular bake). Have ready a 25cm loose-bottomed flan ring set on a baking sheet lined with baking paper.

2 Roll pastry on a lightly floured surface, then line into flan ring. Prick bottom of pastry. Chill.

3 Put hazelnuts in a shallow ovenproof dish and bake for about 12 minutes or until lightly golden. The skins should start peeling back and the nuts will have started to colour. Tip them onto an old clean cloth, bundle them up and rub vigorously to release the skins. Transfer hazelnuts to the bowl of a food processor and process until finely chopped (some bits will remain a little chunky, and that's okay; just be careful not to over-process them or they will turn into an oily paste). If you don't have a food processor, chop very finely by hand.

4 Put butter in a bowl and beat with an electric beater until creamy and loose. Beat in caster sugar a tablespoon at a time and continue beating until fluffy and lighter in colour (creamed; see cooking class on page 111), stopping the machine and scraping down the bowl several times. Beat eggs together with a fork, then add them gradually to the beaten butter and sugar, adding flour halfway through. Mix in orange zest and liqueur, then the hazelnuts and chocolate. Spoon into pastry case and smooth the top.

5 Have a baking sheet heating on a shelf in the lower third of the oven. Slide tart with the baking paper from the cold sheet onto the hot sheet and bake for 30–35 minutes, or until filling is set and pastry golden. Remove tart from oven, cool for 10 minutes, then carefully loosen the sides of the pastry from the flan ring, but leave tart in the flan ring until it cools further.

6 Remove flan ring, slide tart off the base onto a cooling rack and leave until completely cool before serving. Dust with icing sugar to serve.

400g ready-made sweet short pastry, or a 225g batch sweet rich shortcrust pastry (page 76)
225g hazelnuts
90g unsalted butter, cubed and softened
150g caster sugar
2 medium (size 6) free-range eggs, at room temperature
1 Tbsp standard flour
finely grated zest of 1 orange
2 Tbsp orange liqueur, such as Cointreau
90g good-quality dark chocolate with at least 60% cocoa solids, roughly chopped
icing sugar, for dusting

gâteau au chocolat

ready in 45 minutes, plus cooling | serves 8

Dark and rich, sexy and seductive – yep, that's the only way to describe this dessert.

125g good-quality dark chocolate
with at least 70% cocoa solids,
broken into squares or roughly
chopped
100g unsalted butter
50g standard flour
125g caster sugar
4 medium (size 6) free-range eggs,
at room temperature
icing sugar, or icing sugar mixed
with a little cocoa, for dusting
plain unsweetened yoghurt or
crème fraîche, to serve

1 Preheat oven to 190°C (regular bake). Butter sides and base of a 23cm cake tin and line base with baking paper. Shake a little flour around tin to coat sides, then tap out excess.

2 Put chocolate and butter in a bowl and microwave gently until melted (try 30 seconds, stir, then 20 seconds, stir, then 10 seconds). Stir until thoroughly mixed. Alternatively, melt chocolate and butter in a bowl over a saucepan of simmering water, stirring often.

3 Sift flour into a bowl and mix in caster sugar and eggs. Beat briefly with an electric beater on low speed. Stir in chocolate and butter, and mix for 3 minutes until smooth and the mixture forms a thick trail. Spoon into tin.

4 Cook for about 25 minutes (the cake should have coloured on top, and may be a little cracked, but it should still feel softish, not dry, in the centre). Test by piercing with a skewer, which should come out clean. Turn cake out of tin, remove paper then invert onto a cooling rack to cool.

5 Dust cake with icing sugar, or icing sugar and cocoa, cut into slices and serve with yoghurt or crème fraîche.

petits pots de crème

**ready in 35 minutes, plus cooling | serves 6 | makes 2 pots each
of vanilla, coffee and chocolate crème**

*If you want to make more coffee-flavoured or more chocolate crèmes, rather than
vanilla ones, simply use the formula of 1 egg, 1 egg yolk and 1 Tbsp sugar for every
two pots, and increase the amount of coffee or chocolate accordingly.*

1 Preheat oven to 170°C (regular bake).

2 Warm milk in a saucepan with vanilla pod, remove from heat and leave to infuse
for 10 minutes. Remove vanilla pod.

3 Put 1 egg and 1 egg yolk in a bowl and beat with vanilla sugar until blended but
not frothy. Pour on one-third (150ml) of the warm milk. Blend well, then strain
into two little pots or cute ovenproof coffee cups.

4 Using the same bowl, beat 1 egg and 1 yolk with 1 tablespoon of the caster
sugar as above, then blend in 150ml milk and the coffee. Strain into two little
pots.

5 Using the same bowl again, beat the last egg and egg yolk with remaining caster
sugar. Melt chocolate in the remaining milk, then pour onto eggs and sugar.
Strain into 2 little pots.

6 Cover each pot with a round of baking paper then tin foil, and press the foil
around tightly. Stand the pots in water in a shallow roasting tin. Bake for 15–20
minutes until just set – they should wobble just a little when shaken. They can be
served hot, but are more delicious chilled. Dust chocolate pots with cocoa before
serving.

450ml whole milk
½ vanilla pod, split
**3 medium (size 6) free-range eggs,
   plus 3 medium egg yolks**
1 Tbsp vanilla sugar
2 Tbsp caster sugar
2 Tbsp brewed espresso coffee
**60g good-quality dark chocolate
   with at least 60% cocoa solids,
   broken into squares or roughly
   chopped**
cocoa, for dusting

chocolate nut cake

ready in 1 hour, plus cooling | serves at least 8

This cake has been the most popular chocolate cake recipe I've put in print – the video of it has had close to 300,000 hits on YouTube (go to YouTube.com/juliebiuso) and I've received thousands of emails about it. I don't think I need to say any more. Use fresh nuts, as rancid or bitter nuts will spoil the cake; and Valrhona chocolate.

60g unsalted butter

375g good-quality dark chocolate with at least 70% cocoa solids, broken into squares or roughly chopped

80g walnuts, pecans or toasted, skinned hazelnuts (see page 127), plus extra for topping (optional)

45g standard flour

75g caster sugar

2 Tbsp orange liqueur, such as Cointreau

60ml water

6 medium (size 6) free-range eggs, at room temperature

pinch of cream of tartar

lightly whipped cream, for serving

1 Preheat oven to 180°C (regular bake) and set a shelf in the centre of the oven. Line the sides and base of a 23cm cake tin with non-stick baking paper.

2 Put the butter and chocolate in a small saucepan and melt carefully over a low heat, stirring until smooth.

3 Put the nuts, flour and caster sugar in the bowl of a food processor fitted with the chopping blade, or in a blender, and process briefly until the nuts are coarsely ground. Tip nut mixture into a bowl and mix in two-thirds of the melted butter and chocolate mixture, and all the Cointreau and water.

4 Separate eggs, putting the egg whites in a grease-free bowl and the yolks in a small bowl. Beat yolks with a wooden spoon until smooth, then blend into the chocolate mixture. Whip egg whites and cream of tartar together until they form a firm snow, but are not stiff and dry. Mix a large spoonful of the whipped whites into the chocolate mixture, then carefully fold in the rest with a large spoon. Spoon into prepared tin.

5 Bake for 25–30 minutes, or until slightly shrinking from sides of tin and firmish to the touch. Cool in the tin, turn out onto a cooling rack and peel off the paper. Leave until nearly cool (a faint warmth in the cake will help the chocolate topping spread).

6 Gently rewarm the remaining chocolate and butter mixture, then spread over the top and sides of the cake, using a flat-bladed knife, making a pattern similar to that on top of Devil's chocolate cake (page 118). Leave at room temperature until set, but don't refrigerate the cake as the chocolate topping loses its gloss when chilled. If your kitchen is cold and the topping sets and goes dull, revive it with a quick buzz-over with a hair dryer before serving (the warmth should bring back the gloss!). Alternatively, scatter chopped nuts over the topping while still soft. Serve with lightly whipped cream.

A cooking class with Julie

Types of meringue

The word 'meringue' indicates that egg whites and sugar in some proportion are beaten together until a thick foam forms. There are four main types:

- meringue suisse, used for small, crisp meringues
- marshmallow or American meringue, used for pavlova
- meringue cuite, used to form meringue baskets
- Italian meringue, used for patisserie work.

1

2

The two types covered in this book are meringue suisse and marshmallow or American meringue, but I will make brief mention of meringue cuite.

Meringue suisse is a crisp type of meringue, although humidity can make it slightly sticky, and is pale beige in colour with a faintly caramel taste. The egg whites are best when whisked by hand. They are whipped until smooth and shiny and stiff enough to stand unsupported in a peak on the whisk (picture 1). Rotary or electric beaters do not achieve this result as well, because they emulsify the egg white and it becomes too solid. Once the eggs are stiff, 1 teaspoon of sugar per egg is quickly whisked in for less than a minute, then the bulk of the sugar is carefully folded in with a large spoon (picture 2). Care must be taken not to over-mix the meringue when adding the sugar, or it will start to collapse.

Meringue suisse is used for small meringues that can be piped (picture 3) or shaped with spoons. When filling a piping bag with meringue, use a large piping bag to

3

4

minimise deflating the meringue. Fold top of piping bag down, scoop up meringue with a large spoon and lightly transfer it to the piping bag (picture 4). Unfold top of piping bag and gently push meringue down towards nozzle. To pipe, keep the bag upright and gently press the top of the bag. Miniature meringues can be used as a decoration on cakes and gâteaux, and larger ones can be sandwiched together with whipped cream. To ensure two meringue halves will not separate when served, gently bash the smooth side of the meringues with the finger, to give the cream something to grip to. Meringue

5

suisse can also be piped into coils (picture 5) and sandwiched with cream. If filled with cream and then refrigerated, the meringue retains a thin edge of crispness and the rest softens and becomes meltingly tender. Chopped nuts, such as slivered blanched almonds and skinned, toasted chopped hazelnuts, can be folded into the meringue, and the mixture can either be spooned into a high flan ring, which will help it keep its shape, or spooned into a rough round. Both should be put on a baking sheet lined with baking paper to prevent sticking, and can be finished off with cream and fruit once cool.

For meringue suisse, the proportion of sugar to egg white rarely changes from 55g of caster sugar per medium (size 6) egg white. The cooked meringues will keep well for some weeks in an airtight container, providing there is no humidity present. They can also be frozen in a rigid container for 2–3 months.

American meringue is used to make pavlova and is found on top of lemon meringue pies, although sometimes meringue suisse is used for the latter. It has the consistency of marshmallow. It's necessary to use an electric beater because the egg whites and sugar combined are too heavy for a hand whisk (picture 6). Cream of tartar or vinegar is added at the end to cut the grain of the sugar, keeping the meringue soft. Vanilla extract is added to flavour the meringue when making a pavlova (picture 7). The pavlova is spooned out onto a baking sheet lined with baking paper (picture 8)

6

7

8

9

10

11

12

and very lightly shaped into a round. It's essential to use minimal contact to avoid loss of air and deflating the foam (picture 9). The meringue is then ready to be baked (picture 10). It's ready to come out of the oven when the baking paper will peel away without leaving any sticky patches (picture 11). The meringue colours to a pale caramel as it cooks, and spreads very little but rises slightly during cooking. As it cools, it sinks a little and the top cracks; this is quite normal (picture 12). To minimise the cracking, let the pavlova cool in the turned-off oven. The outer shell of a pavlova is crisp and slightly powdery and the inside is a dense marshmallowy foam (picture 13). A pavlova will keep well for several days in an airtight container.

13

Meringue cuite is made with egg white and icing sugar, 55g or more of sugar per medium (size 6) egg white. It is not actually cooked, but can be beaten over a bowl of hot water to help it thicken more quickly; if using a cake mixer, this is not necessary. Meringue cuite will hold its shape after it is made, and it can be used to pipe meringue baskets and other meringue shapes. The texture is dry and powdery and it is often hard; it is also very sweet. It is used for commercially-prepared meringues.

Tips for perfect meringues

Fresh eggs are best for meringues, because the egg white is thick and traps air easily. Egg white thins as the egg ages. Have the eggs at room temperature, because a warm mixture will hold more air than a cold one.

When beating or whisking egg whites, the bowl and beaters must be grease-free, as even a speck of egg yolk can prevent egg whites whipping to a perfect foam. Make sure your hands are washed and grease-free so the egg white does not pick up traces of grease from your hands when you crack the eggs. If a speck of egg yolk accidentally gets in the bowl, scoop it out with a clean piece of eggshell. When separating eggs, have three bowls: a small grease-free bowl for putting each egg white into as the eggs are separated; a bowl for the yolks; and the grease-free bowl for whipping the egg whites. Transfer the egg whites to the whipping bowl one at a time as the eggs are cracked. This way, should you accidentally break a yolk when cracking an egg and contaminate the egg white, you are only messing up that one egg (put it into a separate container, refrigerate and use in an omelette or similar).

Start beating on a slow speed, as the aim is to build as many small bubbles as possible. Once a soft foam forms, increase the speed. Sugar should not be added until the foam has formed, not until at least halfway through beating. Use caster sugar as it breaks down easily with beating. Coarse sugar can hold moisture and can cause the meringue to 'weep' after cooking. Undissolved sugar also causes meringues to weep as they cool. Once sugar is folded or beaten in, the foam is more stable.

Egg whites will not whisk well in a plastic bowl, even if it is clean and appears grease-free. A copper bowl is best for meringue suisse, because the foam is creamier and more stable. A chemical reaction takes place where the egg white protein combines with the copper in the bowl to form a new protein, resulting in a more stable foam. There is also less chance of over-beating egg whites when using a copper bowl, and of having them collapse; once the eggs and sugar are stiff, the meringue will hold for 15–30 minutes. If using a glass or china bowl, a pinch of cream of tartar helps the egg whites to denature and will help stabilise the foam.

14

The bowl and whisk must be grease-free before use, and a copper bowl needs special cleaning preparation. Clean the inside of a copper bowl with a quarter of a lemon, slightly flattened, and 2 tablespoons of kitchen salt. Rub the salt around the bowl using the lemon (picture 14). Then rinse clean and shake dry, or wipe with paper towels. A copper bowl must be prepared this way each time, or you might find your egg whites take on a green tinge. In place of lemon, white vinegar can be used. After use, the bowl should be washed in warm water and dried. If the whisk needs to be washed in soapy water, rinse it thoroughly under running hot water to make sure it is free of detergent.

Whisk the egg whites slowly to begin with, using a loose wrist motion. Once foamy, increase the speed and use an exaggerated whipping motion to incorporate as much air as possible. As soon as the egg whites are stiff enough to hold their shape on the upturned whisk, they are ready (see picture 1, page 134). Prolonged beating will cause the egg whites to become dry and brittle.

Egg whites are also beaten to a foam without sugar, then folded into cakes, mousses, soufflés and the like to lighten them.

- For a soft foam, to use as a glaze, beat with a fork or small metal whisk.

- For a firm snow or soft peaks, where the whipped whites barely support themselves and flop over off the beater (to incorporate into cakes, soufflés and mousses), use a small metal whisk or a large balloon whisk and a copper, metal or china bowl; or a rotary or hand-held electric beater.

- For stiff peaks, for meringues, use a large balloon whisk and a copper, metal or china bowl, or a hand-held electric beater or large cake mixer with a whisking attachment.

- Pavlova-style meringues must always be beaten with an electric beater; a large cake mixer with a whisking beater is ideal.

Don't bang beaters on the side of the bowl or you'll knock out air; instead, bang them on your hand.

festive

three-berry fool

ready in 30 minutes, plus chilling time | serves 6–8

Fruit fools are deceptively rich, so serve small portions at the end of a light meal. Even so, the ratio of fruit to cream and custard needs to be high to avoid the fool being bland and overly rich. Strawberries alone in a fool are bland, but raspberries improve flavour and colour. Sieve the berries to catch the bits that would interfere with the creamy texture. This fool works best with homemade custard – it can be made with custard using custard powder, but will lack the gorgeous velvety texture.

1 Make the custard according to the recipe on page 97.

2 Put half the fruit with the lemon juice in a food processor bowl or in a liquidiser. Process until smooth. Push the purée through a sieve into a bowl.

3 When the custard is cool, whip cream until stiff. Chop the rest of the strawberries. Blend custard and cream together, then partially stir in fruit purée, raspberries, blackberries and chopped strawberries, leaving the mixture streaky. Spoon into glasses and chill for 2–3 hours. Garnish with a few chopped berries before serving.

one batch homemade custard (page 97), using triple the amount of arrowroot (i.e. 3 level tsp)

300g strawberries, hulled and sliced

300g raspberries (frozen raspberries can be used)

150g blackberries

1 Tbsp lemon juice

200ml cream

a few extra berries, to serve

hazelnut and raspberry ice cream cake

ready in 40 minutes, plus freezing | serves 8–12

Hazelnuts, raspberries, chocolate and grog – how can this fail to bring you a round of appreciative applause? All you have to remember is to remove it from the freezer and place it in the refrigerator 1 hour before serving (get it made in advance for a hassle-free dinner party dessert).

300g raspberries

1 Tbsp icing sugar, plus extra for dusting

300g lady finger biscuits (also known as boudoir biscuits or sponge fingers)

250ml coffee, Frangelico or chocolate liqueur (you may need a little more)

4 medium (size 6) free-range egg yolks, at room temperature

100g caster sugar

300ml cream, lightly whipped

150g mascarpone

1½ tsp vanilla extract

60g toasted, skinned hazelnuts (see page 127), chopped

50g good-quality dark chocolate with at least 60% cocoa solids, coarsely grated

1 Put half the raspberries in a bowl and carefully stir through 1 tablespoon of icing sugar. Leave for 30 minutes, stirring occasionally.

2 Line a 23cm diameter by 4cm deep cake tin with plastic food wrap. Cut most of the lady fingers in half to form two short pieces. Steep in liqueur for 1 minute, then remove to a plate. Line sides of tin with biscuits, rounded end facing down. To hold these in place, wedge whole biscuits on base. Once sides are secure, remove biscuits from base, steep in liqueur then place, sugar side down, to line base of tin. Plug any gaps with small pieces of biscuit.

3 In a bowl, whisk egg yolks and caster sugar together until pale and very thick (about 7 minutes). In a separate bowl, gently mix cream into mascarpone. Fold cream and mascarpone into egg yolks and sugar, along with vanilla extract, hazelnuts, chocolate and sweetened raspberries. Spoon mixture into tin. Freeze.

4 Once dessert is set, layer the top with more biscuits dunked in liqueur. Cover and return to the freezer. Before serving, transfer to the refrigerator for 1 hour to soften.

5 To serve, invert cake onto serving plate, remove tin and plastic food wrap. Put a mound of raspberries in the centre of the cake and dust them with icing sugar.

big fruit cake

ready in 2 hours, plus cooling | makes a big cake, serves 20

This delicious cake is based on a recipe by British chef Gary Rhodes. He uses whisky in his but I prefer brandy, and I've added chunks of chocolate for an element of surprise.

1 Put dried fruit and glacé cherries in a bowl with the lemon zest, lemon juice and brandy, stir well, cover and leave to soften for 1 hour (or up to 12 hours).

2 Preheat oven to 170°C (regular bake). Line bottom and sides of a 20cm deep cake tin with baking paper.

3 Sift flour, baking powder, cinnamon, mixed spice and salt together on a piece of paper.

4 Put butter in a bowl and beat briefly with an electric beater until creamy and loose. Beat in caster sugar a tablespoon at a time and continue beating until fluffy and lighter in colour (creamed; see cooking class on page 111). You'll need to stop the machine and scrape down the sides of the bowl several times. Beat eggs together with a fork, then add them gradually to the creamed butter and sugar, adding a tablespoon or two of the sifted dry ingredients to help stabilise the mixture.

5 Fold in remaining sifted dry ingredients, ground almonds, dried and glacé fruit with all the juices, and the chocolate. Mix in milk. Spoon cake mix into tin, and smooth the top with a knife. Scatter almonds on top or make a pattern with them.

6 Bake for about 1½ hours, protecting the top of the cake with tin foil after the first hour. When the cake is done, a skewer inserted in the centre should come out clean. Cool in the tin, then, keeping cake in its baking paper, wrap in greaseproof paper. Store in an airtight container (uncut, the cake will keep well for a few weeks but once cut, it will dry out in several days).

160g currants
160g sultanas
50g glacé cherries, chopped
finely grated zest and juice of 2 lemons
3 Tbsp brandy
200g high-grade flour
1 tsp baking powder
¼ tsp ground cinnamon
½ tsp mixed spice
pinch of salt
175g unsalted butter, cubed and softened
175g caster sugar
3 large (size 7) free-range eggs
2 Tbsp ground almonds
100g dark unsweetened chocolate, cut into small cubes
100ml milk, at room temperature
70g blanched almonds, for the top

quick panettone trifles

ready in 20 minutes | serves 4–6

Panettone is a dome-shaped cake with a light texture and buttery taste, studded with peel and dried fruit, or sometimes chocolate, nuts and sugar. Popular as a Christmas cake with coffee, tea or bubbly, it can also be used to make other desserts. Reputably, there was a Milanese baker in the 15th century called Toni, whose beautiful daughter captured the heart of a young aristocrat whose family forbade the union. The gentleman would visit the daughter in the bakery where she worked at night, and when her father, the baker Toni, fell on hard times, he helped out with supplies, adding butter and sugar to the dough, which made it richer and sweeter. It quickly became popular, and the wealthy ladies of Milan came flocking. Toni got rich, meaning the young couple could marry after all and they all lived happily ever after.

250g strawberries

2 Tbsp caster sugar

4 Tbsp Frangelico liqueur, or liqueur of your choice

4 Tbsp espresso (or strong plunger coffee)

200g panettone, cubed

200ml cream

finely grated zest of 1 lemon, and 1 Tbsp lemon juice

ready-made chocolate sauce (optional)

60g toasted roughly chopped hazelnuts

1 Hull and slice the strawberries and put them in a bowl with 1 tablespoon of the caster sugar. Mix carefully, then leave at room temperature for 15–20 minutes until the juices run.

2 Mix liqueur and coffee in a small ramekin. Put cubed panettone on a large plate and spoon over coffee and liqueur.

3 Whip the cream with the other tablespoon of sugar until it holds its shape, but don't let it get stiff or it will become buttery. Then fold through lemon zest and juice.

4 Assemble trifles in glasses, layering panettone cubes, cream and strawberries. Finish with a layer of cream and strawberries, drizzle with a little chocolate sauce if liked, and sprinkle hazelnuts over. The trifles can be served straight away or refrigerated for up to 1 hour before serving.

choux pastry tree with white chocolate and raspberries

ready in 2 hours (or more if you need to make a mould) | serves 12

Aluminium croquembouche cones can be hired to make this dessert, otherwise make a cone out of stiff card and cover it with heavy-duty tin foil. Make two batches of choux pastry to get the required number of buns – you'll need about 100.

1 Preheat oven to 180°C (regular bake). Prepare cone if necessary and put it on a baking sheet lined with baking paper to catch drips and to make it easy to move.

2 To make choux buns (see cooking class on page 162), sift flour with a pinch of salt onto a piece of paper. Put water and butter in a roomy saucepan and heat gently until butter melts. Bring to a rolling boil, remove pan from heat, shoot in flour in one go and beat vigorously until the ingredients are combined and the mixture comes away from the sides of the pan. As soon as it does, stop beating. Cool.

3 Lightly beat eggs with a large pinch of salt. When the paste is cool, add eggs a little at a time, beating after each addition, until the paste is smooth and glossy (use a hand-held electric beater).

4 Line a baking sheet with baking paper and splash with a few beads of water. Fit a large piping bag with a small (1cm) plain nozzle and fill with choux paste. Pipe small rounds onto baking sheet. Alternatively, simply use two spoons to scoop and push off small amounts of choux paste onto prepared sheets.

5 Transfer to a shelf in the top third of oven, then immediately increase heat to 200°C. Bake until crisp and brown, about 20–25 minutes, then slide off baking sheet onto a cooling rack. Pierce each bun on the side with a skewer to let the steam escape. Cool. Repeat with remaining choux paste.

6 Crush raspberries until there are no lumps. Whip cream with icing sugar until nice and thick, then swirl raspberries through. Fill buns using a teaspoon, or a large piping bag with a small (1cm) plain nozzle. Take a bun in your hand and gently prise it open enough to fill with cream.

7 When all buns are filled, assemble the tree. Melt chocolate. Slip a freezer pack in the centre of the cone – to help the chocolate set and hold the buns in place. One by one, smear undersides of buns generously with chocolate and stick them onto the cone, starting at the base. When cone is completely covered, dribble chocolate over the buns from the end of a teaspoon. Dust with icing sugar (a tea strainer is best for this), then sprinkle with silver balls – I simply threw a handful of them at the choux tree, and left them where they landed. To serve, guests gently prise off each bun. The chocolate behind each bun stays on the cone. Leftover buns can be removed from the cone and refrigerated for up to 2 days.

choux buns (single batch)
100g high-grade flour
salt
215ml water
85g unsalted butter
3 medium (size 6) free-range eggs

to finish
200g fresh or frozen raspberries
375ml cream
1 Tbsp icing sugar, plus extra for dusting
300g white chocolate
silver balls, to decorate (optional)

pavlova with greek yoghurt and raspberries

ready in 1 hour 30 minutes, plus cooling | serves 8–10

It might be hard to believe until you try this, but using Greek yoghurt in place of cream turns pavlova into a luxurious velvety treat (and one with fewer calories). I warn you – one piece will not be enough!

4 medium (size 6) free-range egg whites, at room temperature

pinch of salt

225g caster sugar (smooth out any lumps with a spoon)

2 tsp cornflour

1 tsp white vinegar

½ tsp vanilla extract

topping

500g Greek-style honey yoghurt

300g raspberries

icing sugar, for dusting

1 Preheat oven to 120°C (regular bake).

2 Put egg whites and salt in a grease-free bowl, and whisk egg whites with an electric beater until stiff (see cooking class on page 134). Continue whisking while adding caster sugar a tablespoon at a time. Whisk for several minutes more until very stiff, then turn off machine and sprinkle cornflour, vinegar and vanilla extract over. Use a large metal spoon to carefully mix ingredients together without deflating the whipped whites.

3 Transfer mixture in dollops to a baking sheet lined with baking paper and shape into a rough round, about 20cm in diameter – don't try to make it perfect and smooth because you'll knock out air.

4 Bake in oven for 1 hour, by which time the meringue should be crisp on the top; it may be slightly sunken under the crisp shell, but this is normal. Turn oven off and leave pavlova in oven for at least 1 hour but preferably until the oven is cool (overnight is fine; just remember to remove it before you start the oven again!).

5 Just before serving, carefully peel away baking paper from underneath pavlova and transfer pavlova to a cake plate. Beat yoghurt until smooth, then put dollops of yoghurt on top of the pavlova. Strew with raspberries, then either leave at room temperature for up to 2 hours or transfer to the refrigerator. Dust raspberries with icing sugar before serving. I think the pavlova is at its best about 4–8 hours after assembling, by which time it has softened and is no longer brittle, but the outer shell still has a gorgeous crunch.

almond macaroons

ready in 45 minutes | makes 30

These gorgeously chewy macaroons will keep quite well in an airtight container for 3–4 days.

200g caster sugar

30g granulated sugar

115g ground almonds

1 Tbsp rice flour (available from large supermarkets or health food stores)

2–3 egg whites, depending on size

3 drops vanilla extract

split almonds, for the top

1 Preheat oven to 160°C (regular bake).

2 In a bowl, mix sugars, ground almonds and rice flour. Add egg whites and vanilla extract. Beat together with an electric beater for 2 minutes (mixture should be loose but not thick; add extra egg white if necessary). Scrape down sides of bowl, rest mixture for 5 minutes, then beat for 3–5 minutes until thick and white.

3 Using a piping bag and a small (1cm) plain nozzle, pipe neat shapes onto a baking sheet lined with baking paper and place a split almond in the centre of each. Bake for 20–30 minutes, or until pale gold in colour. Cool for a few minutes on the paper, then carefully peel off the paper and cool on a cooling rack. Store in an airtight container as soon as they are cool.

ricotta hotcakes with strawberries and maple syrup

ready in 30 minutes | makes 24

Try these for a festive brunch – the lightness of fluffy ricotta hotcakes, strawberries and maple syrup makes them memorable.

4 large (size 7) free-range eggs

200g ricotta

pinch of salt

finely grated zest of 1 lemon

2 Tbsp unsalted butter, melted

5 level Tbsp standard flour

2 Tbsp caster sugar

250g strawberries, hulled and
  sliced

1 Tbsp icing sugar

sliced banana, maple syrup, cream
  or yoghurt, to serve

1 Separate eggs, putting whites in a grease-free bowl. Put egg yolks in a large bowl and beat with a wooden spoon until smooth and liquid. Beat in ricotta, salt and lemon zest. Pour in melted butter, then work in flour.

2 Whisk egg whites until stiff peaks form, then beat in caster sugar and continue beating for 2–3 minutes until glossy. Using a large spoon, mix 1 large spoonful of whipped egg whites into the ricotta mixture, then carefully fold in the rest.

3 Heat a lightly buttered non-stick frying pan over gentle heat, or preheat a lightly greased barbecue hot plate. Working in batches, drop spoonfuls of batter onto hot pan or hot plate, making hotcakes about 6cm in diameter. Cook for 1–2 minutes, until golden, then flip and cook the other side. Transfer to a cooling rack as they are done, and cover with a clean tea towel.

4 Mix strawberries with icing sugar. Serve the hotcakes with strawberries, banana, maple syrup and cream or yoghurt.

frangipane mince pies

ready in 45 minutes | makes 24

Love mince pies but looking for a new twist? Here's something different that's at once familiar, but also surprising. They'll keep in an airtight container for several days. If you prefer, they can be gently rewarmed before serving.

100g dried apricots

125ml boiling water

400g fruit mince

finely grated zest of 1 lemon

½ tsp ground cinnamon

¼ tsp mixed spice

70g flaked almonds, toasted

3 pre-rolled frozen sheets sweet
   shortcrust pastry about 24cm x
   24cm, thawed just before using

frangipane

100g unsalted butter, softened

100g caster sugar

1 Tbsp standard flour

2 large (size 7) free-range eggs,
   lightly beaten

100g ground almonds

apricot glaze

1 small jar inexpensive apricot jam

1 Tbsp lemon juice

1 Put apricots in a bowl, pour on boiling water and leave to soften for 2–3 hours. Drain and chop. Mix in a bowl with fruit mince, lemon zest, cinnamon, mixed spice and half the flaked almonds.

2 To make the frangipane, whip butter and sugar together in a food processor until light and fluffy. Scrape down the sides of the bowl and add the flour. With the machine running, gradually whip in the eggs, then the ground almonds. Alternatively, use an electric beater.

3 Preheat oven to 190°C (fanbake). Cut pastry into 24 rounds with an 8cm ring cutter and line into shallow muffin trays (you may need to cook the mince pies in batches).

4 Spoon in fruit mixture and top each with a tablespoon of frangipane. Spread it over the fruit with the back of the spoon (you don't need to be too pedantic about this as it will soften and spread as it heats). Sprinkle with remaining flaked almonds. Bake for about 15 minutes, or until the pastry and topping are golden.

5 To make the apricot glaze, heat apricot jam in a small saucepan with lemon juice. Bring to the boil, stirring, then pass it through a metal sieve and discard lumps. The glaze, while hot, should drop from a spoon and leave the spoon coated. Thin it with a little water if necessary, or bubble it to reduce it if it's too thin. When ready to use the glaze, reheat it to boiling point and apply it while it is very hot.

6 Brush mince pies with bubbling-hot apricot glaze, cool in the tins for 5 minutes, then remove from tins and cool on a cooling rack. Store the pies in an airtight container once cool.

eton mess with a twist

ready in: meringue prep 15 minutes, plus 3 hours baking and cooling, plus 20 minutes to assemble, plus chilling | serves 8

You can make Eton Mess up to five days in advance and freeze it in a rigid container. Limoncello (lemon liqueur) stops this scrumptious mixture from freezing solid. You can make it with leftover meringues, or make a fresh batch as described below. The meringues can be used in other desserts – they're especially gorgeous sandwiched with whipped cream, or whipped cream and lemon curd together, and served with fresh strawberries or other berries.

1 Preheat oven to 130°C (regular bake). Line two baking sheets with baking paper.

2 To make meringues, whisk egg whites in a totally grease-free bowl until they are stiff and can stand in peaks on an upturned whisk (see cooking class on page 135). Add 2 tablespoons caster sugar and whisk in for 30 seconds. Sprinkle the rest of the caster sugar over and fold it in carefully with a large metal spoon.

3 Put meringue in a piping bag fitted with a small (1cm) plain nozzle and pipe shapes onto the baking sheets. Alternatively, use two small spoons to shape blobs of meringue on the baking sheets. Bake meringues for at least 1 hour, or until crisp and they will lift off the paper without feeling tacky. Swap the positions of the baking sheets during cooking.

4 Tap a little hole in the base of each meringue with a skewer and return meringues to the turned-off oven to dry out; leave for 1–2 hours if possible, then store in an airtight container.

5 When ready to assemble dessert, crush half the raspberries with a fork. Whip cream in a large bowl, then crumble in three-quarters of the meringues. Gently mix meringues through the cream, then stir in half the limoncello and all the crushed raspberries. Crumble in the rest of the meringues and gently fold together. Transfer to a container and freeze.

6 Hull and slice half the strawberries. Mix in a bowl with 1 tablespoon icing sugar and the remaining limoncello. Cover and refrigerate. Hull remaining strawberries, chop roughly and purée in a food processor. Add a squeeze of lemon juice.

7 To serve, put scoops of Eton mess in glasses, top with strawberries and spoon over a little strawberry purée. Dust remaining raspberries with icing sugar and arrange on top of the desserts. Serve immediately.

3 medium (size 6) free-range egg whites, at room temperature
165g caster sugar
150g fresh or frozen raspberries
400ml cream
125ml limoncello liqueur
500g strawberries
1 Tbsp icing sugar, plus extra for dusting
lemon juice

choux buns with strawberries and cream

ready in 45 minutes, plus cooling | makes 12

Pretty as a picture – the trick with these is to have a miserly touch with the pink colouring because lurid pink icing is a killer. I use a bamboo skewer for the job and drip in a few 'dots' (not as big as a drop!) at a time. It's wise to line the workbench with plastic food wrap in case of splashes. Other berries, such as blackberries and raspberries, and seasonal fruit, can also be used in place of strawberries in these choux buns

1 Preheat oven to 180°C (regular bake).

2 For choux paste (see cooking class on page 162), sift flour with a pinch of salt onto a piece of paper. Put water and butter in a roomy saucepan and heat gently until butter melts. Bring to a rolling boil, remove pan from the heat, shoot in the flour in one go and beat vigorously until the ingredients are combined and the mixture comes away from the sides of the pan. As soon as it does that, stop beating. Cool.

3 Lightly beat eggs with a large pinch of salt. When the paste is cool, add eggs a little at a time, beating well after each addition, until the mixture is smooth and glossy (easily done with a hand-held electric beater).

4 Line a baking sheet with baking paper and splash with a few beads of water. Fit a large piping bag with a large (2cm) fluted nozzle and fill with choux paste. Pipe 12 rosettes onto the baking sheets. Alternatively, use two spoons to scoop and push off spoonfuls of choux paste onto prepared sheet. Transfer to the top third of the oven, then immediately increase heat to 200°C. Bake until crisp and brown, about 20–25 minutes, then slide off baking sheet onto a cooling rack. Cut a lid from each choux bun and leave to cool. (If the buns are still a little gooey in the centre, return them to the turned-off oven for 5 minutes to dry out.)

5 Hull and slice strawberries and put them in a bowl with 1 tablespoon of the icing sugar and a splash of limoncello, if using. Whip cream with the other tablespoon of icing sugar. Fill buns with cream, then spoon in strawberries. Put tops of choux buns in place. Either dust with icing sugar or drizzle with pink icing. Serve within 30 minutes.

6 To make pink icing, put icing sugar in a bowl and stir in lemon juice in two to three lots. When the icing is smooth, add a few dots of food colouring; add a very small amount to begin with (once it's in, it can't be taken out or diluted) and beat in thoroughly. If not using immediately, cover surface of icing with plastic food wrap, and beat again before using. Use the day of making.

choux paste
100g high-grade flour
salt
215ml water
85g unsalted butter
3 medium (size 6) free-range eggs

fruit and cream
250–300g strawberries
2 Tbsp icing sugar (plus extra for sifting over finished buns if required)
splash of limoncello liqueur (optional)
300ml cream

pink icing
320g icing sugar, sifted
50ml lemon juice, strained
pink food colouring

rhubarb, vanilla and ginger fool

ready in 40 minutes | serves 4

This fool is light and tangy with fewer calories than a conventional fool made with cream and custard. When buying rhubarb, look for uncut stalks that have been pulled from the plant, not cut. The stalk ends should be fleshy and firm, and not feel slimy. Stalks, too, should be firm, not spongy or withered. Look for red stalks, rather than those with too much green, because they are sweeter and less astringent. Size is not a guide; big stalks can be just as tender as little ones.

750g rhubarb

75g vanilla sugar, or use caster sugar and the seeds from half a vanilla pod

1 piece fresh root ginger about the size of a walnut, peeled and thinly sliced

750ml plain unsweetened yoghurt

125ml Greek-style honey yoghurt

sweet biscuits to serve (optional)

1 Preheat oven to 180°C (fanbake).

2 Wash rhubarb well, then trim and cut into short lengths. Transfer to a shallow ovenproof dish. Sprinkle vanilla sugar over and distribute ginger amongst rhubarb. Cover tightly with tin foil, then bake for 20 minutes until nicely tender.

3 Cool rhubarb, then tilt dish and let juices run into one corner of dish. Scoop off juices and reserve. Put rhubarb and some ginger slices (add according to taste) in a liquidiser and blend until puréed. Pour in the plain yoghurt and blend.

4 Layer the rhubarb and yoghurt mixture into four glasses or fancy dishes with blobs of Greek-style honey yoghurt and drizzles of rhubarb juice. Put aside a little honey yoghurt and rhubarb juice until ready to serve. If not serving immediately, cover and refrigerate until required. Before serving, put a small blob of honey yoghurt on top of each dessert and spoon a little rhubarb juice over the top. If you like, serve with sweet biscuits.

summer fruit salad with sugared yoghurt cream

ready in 15 minutes, plus 8 hours steeping | serves 8

This is so simple, yet so scrumptious. The sugars seep into the yoghurt cream as the dessert chills overnight, and form a crust on top. It's utterly gorgeous. Choose locally grown strawberries because they will always beat imported ones for flavour. Varieties selected for local markets are more likely to be chosen for their ripening ability, colour, juice and taste, whereas imported varieties will have been chosen to withstand temperature change, travel and storage.

250g strawberries

4 perfectly ripe peaches or nectarines

1 passionfruit

250g raspberries

sugared yoghurt cream

300ml cream

2 cups thick Greek-style yoghurt

brown sugar

demerara sugar

1 Hull strawberries and slice. Peel and slice peaches or nectarines. Put fruit in a serving bowl with the pulp of the passionfruit and the raspberries.

2 Whip cream until stiff. Spoon yoghurt into a bowl, whisk until smooth, then fold through the cream. Spoon onto the fruit in dollops. Sprinkle thickly with brown sugar, then with demerara sugar, completely covering the top of the cream. Cover with plastic food wrap and refrigerate for at least 8 hours (but no more than 24 hours) before serving.

A cooking class with Julie

Choux pastry

Choux pastry has a different set of rules to that of other pastry. When it is raw it is more like a paste than a dough, and when it is cooked it forms a crisp hollow shell with a thin layer of soft interior paste. It should be as light as the proverbial feather. It's reasonably quick and easy to make, but care must be taken to weigh and measure ingredients accurately.

Traditionally, it is the pastry used for éclairs, profiteroles and cream puffs. It can also be used in savoury dishes and can be baked and fried. Milk can replace some of the water in the paste, or chicken or vegetable stock for savoury choux dishes.

1

2

3

To make, butter and water (or other liquid) are put into a deep-sided saucepan which allows plenty of space to beat vigorously once the eggs are added. The butter is gently melted (picture 1), then the butter and water are quickly brought to a rolling boil; the water must not boil before the butter has melted, or it will reduce and may therefore be insufficient in volume. As soon as the water comes to a rolling boil, the pan is removed from the heat (or the heat underneath is turned off) and the flour is immediately added in one lot and quickly beaten in (pictures 2 and 3); the water must be boiling rapidly when the flour is added to ensure it cooks through.

4

The ingredients are beaten only until they leave the sides of the pan and come together as a soft smooth paste – this takes a matter of seconds (picture 4). Continued beating at this stage makes the paste oily, which prevents the pastry from holding air and rising properly and, when cooked, it will have a cake-like texture. The paste is then left to cool (it can be turned out onto a plate to cool more quickly), then returned to the saucepan. If eggs are added to the hot paste they may start to cook. However, the paste should not be left until completely cold. It is better to use it warm, as anything that is warm will hold more air than if it is cold.

Strong or high-grade flour with a high gluten content gives the most crisp result. The flour must be dry and sifted with a pinch of salt, to aerate. Sift it onto a piece of paper so that it is easy to shoot it into the boiling water and butter in one go.

Beat the eggs together with a pinch of salt to help break down the albumen. The

5

6

7

eggs can then be dribbled in gradually (picture 5). Once you start adding the egg it is impossible to overbeat (you can switch to an electric beater for this job). Learn to recognise when the paste has taken the maximum amount of egg: it will be yellow, smooth and glossy, not stiff as in the beginning, but still stiff enough to hold its shape with just a slight softening around the edges (picture 6). Medium-sized eggs are best. If eggs are large, keep back one egg white. If too much egg is added, the paste will be difficult to form into shapes and will spread during baking. Once all the egg is added, the pastry should be thoroughly beaten for 1 minute.

Scoop up a small spoonful of paste and use a second spoon to push it off onto a baking sheet lined with baking paper (picture 7). Don't worry unduly about the shape of the buns, as they rise and puff and loosely resemble little heads of cabbage once cooked (choux is 'cabbage' in French). Alternatively, fill the mixture into a piping bag and pipe into shapes.

Choux pastry is baked in the centre of a hot oven on a rising temperature, which means the oven temperature is set below the required cooking temperature, then when the pastry is put in the oven the temperature is increased. The increase in temperature helps the pastry puff up. Flick the baking sheet with a little water before putting it in the oven. It turns to steam and also helps the pastry puff up.

Do not open the oven door until at least three-quarters of the cooking time has elapsed. A sudden drop in temperature before the pastry is baked in position will cause it to collapse; likewise if you remove the choux buns from the oven before they are cooked in position.

Choux pastry must be baked until crisp and brown – yellow patches are a sign of undercooked pastry. Undercooked pastry will quickly turn soft and shapes such as buns will collapse.

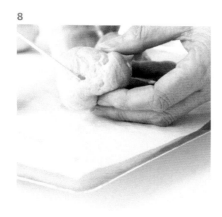

8

For choux buns or éclairs, remove them from the baking sheet and make a small hole in the side with a skewer so steam can escape (picture 8). This will help keep them crisp. If they are gooey inside, return them to the turned-off oven to dry further. Cream can then be piped into this small hole using a piping bag and nozzle.

Raw choux paste can be kept in the refrigerator for a day or two; bring to room temperature before using. Once cooked, it does not keep well, although small choux buns can be kept in a thick brown paper bag at room temperature for 24 hours, providing it is not humid. The paper absorbs the moisture and helps keep the choux buns crisp. Cooked unfilled choux buns can be frozen.

Using a piping bag

1

2

If using a piping bag to make choux buns, use a 1cm (½-inch) piping nozzle for small shapes, and a 2cm (1-inch) piping nozzle for larger buns.

If you are right-handed, put the piping bag in your left hand and roll it down to form a cuff. Scoop the choux paste into the piping bag (picture 1), filling the bag no more than two-thirds full. Unroll the cuff and squeeze the bag from the top of the paste to shoot it down towards the piping nozzle (picture 2), twisting the top of the bag to prevent mixture coming out the top. When more mixture needs to be added, roll back the cuff again and fill as described. Reverse these instructions if you are left-handed. Use a similar method for filling choux buns or éclairs, or piping meringues.

Using the warming or melting method

This is one of the easier cake-making methods, requiring little more than a saucepan, a bowl and a wooden spoon. It's perfect for cooks who can't stand flour under the fingernails (rubbing-in method), or who always curdle creamed mixtures. It is used for gingerbreads and some cakes, notably fruit cakes, and produces baking with a moist and sticky texture that improves with keeping. A high proportion of raising agents is often called for as eggs are not always included or, when they are, they are not sufficient in number to raise the batter on their own.

1

2

The fat, usually butter, is warmed with sugar or syrup (picture 1) and sometimes also with the liquid (or part of it) called for in the recipe, until the butter melts and the sugar dissolves or the syrup liquefies (picture 2). The temperature should be just sufficient to melt or loosen the ingredients. The melted mixture is cooled before stirring into the dry ingredients. If poured in hot it would start to cook the flour, making the finished cake tough. However, cold ingredients such as milk and egg cool it down sufficiently, so the recipe can be continued without a long pause; or, if the cold ingredients are poured into a well in the dry ingredients first and the warmed ingredients poured in after, the mixture will remain cool. Stir just to mix; don't beat (pictures 3 and 4). The batter is thinner than most other cake mixtures and is poured into the prepared tin, finding its own level.

3

4

For the spiced ginger roll on page 73, line a Swiss roll tin with a paper case to make it easy to remove the cake from the tin. Place a piece of baking paper inside the tin and mark out the creases by pressing with a finger. Then, on the work surface, make the creases more definite. Mitre the corners together and secure with metal paper clips (picture 5). Slip the paper case inside the Swiss roll tin.

5

glossary and food tips

arrowroot

The dried root of a tropical plant, this is ground to make a nutritious powdery starch, which is then used to thicken sweet and savoury dishes. It is preferable in many cases to cornflour because it clears on boiling; cornflour becomes cloudy. Add arrowroot dissolved in a little water to the liquid and bring up to the boil – and boil for 30 seconds only, to cook the starch through, unless directed otherwise in the recipe. Continued boiling will cause it to lose its thickening properties (the reverse is true with liquids thickened with cornflour, which become thicker with prolonged boiling).

baking powder and bicarbonate of soda

baking powder – is a mixture of a mild acid, usually cream of tartar, and a mild alkali, usually bicarbonate of soda, that forms a chemical reaction when wetted. The effervescing is caused by carbon dioxide gas forming, which causes baking to rise. Any mixture containing baking powder *must* be cooked straight after mixing to utilise its full potential. Replace it on a regular basis – it will keep fresh for about 12 months.

bicarbonate of soda – is more commonly known as baking soda.

blueberries

The overall antioxidant rating of blueberries is excellent, so that, and their great taste and versatility, gives plenty of reason to include them in the diet. A squeeze of lemon enhances their fruitiness, making them sweeter. They are also one of the few berries that freeze well.

brûlée

French word meaning 'burnt'. Used to describe dishes with a caramel topping.

butter

Used in cake making to give a soft texture and a good flavour, and to improve the keeping qualities (see page 111). Unsalted butter is used throughout this book because salted butter varies in salt content and can affect the flavour of some baking. Often a pinch of salt is added for flavour or to draw out the flavour of other ingredients.

buttermilk

Originally the term used to describe the liquid residue of milk or cream after it was churned to make butter. These days, 'cultured' buttermilk is made by adding a natural culture to standard skimmed milk. Using buttermilk for baking – think scones and hotcakes – makes it lighter and adds a pleasant tang. For a good substitute, add a few squirts of lemon juice to milk and leave it at room temperature for 30 minutes – it won't have quite the full nutty-sour taste of buttermilk, but it will be very close.

cherries

Look for nice plump, smooth and shiny-skinned, blemish-free fruit, with green or supple stalks. Store cherries with the stalks to help them stay fresh. Eat any cherries with nicks or damaged skins soon after purchase and remove any soft or rotting cherries because one bad cherry can quickly spoil others it is close to. Store cherries in the refrigerator – they deteriorate quickly at room temperature. Don't wash cherries until you are ready to use them, as moisture causes them to decay.

chocolate

You will have great success with the chocolate recipes in this book using Valrhona chocolate, which has around 64% cocoa solids; otherwise use bittersweet chocolate with between 55% and 75% cocoa solids.

To melt chocolate, break into squares or chop roughly. Put in a heatproof bowl set over a saucepan with a little simmering water in it, ensuring the bottom of the bowl doesn't touch the water. Turn off the heat – the heat of the water will be sufficient to melt the chocolate – and stir until chocolate has melted, ensuring no water vapour or drips of water come in contact with the chocolate, as this could cause the chocolate to seize, making it unusable. As soon as it has melted, remove bowl from the heat and dry the bottom of the bowl. Alternatively, melt gently in a microwave on medium-high power, in short bursts, stirring often.

condensed milk

'Condensed milk' and 'sweetened condensed milk' refer to the same product – milk which has had water removed and sugar added.

cornflour

In the United States this is known as cornstarch, and is starch extracted from corn (maize) kernels. Do not substitute corn flour, which is ground from dried corn kernels.

cream cheese

Made from cow's milk, with about 35% fat. It has a smooth, soft texture ideal for baked cheesecakes. Low-fat versions are available but are often unsuitable for baking; it is better to mix cream cheese with lower-fat dairy products like ricotta or sour cream.

crème fraîche

Similar to sour cream but with about 30% fat instead of 20%. The higher fat content means crème fraîche is less likely to curdle when heated.

curdle

Intended coagulation, as in scrambled eggs; or accidental, as when adding eggs to creamed butter and sugar. Curdled mixtures may sometimes be 'rescued' (see page 112).

desiccated coconut

Coconut with the moisture removed. To prolong the freshness of desiccated coconut, store it in a container in the freezer.

digestive biscuits

These are known as Graham crackers in the United States and Canada.

dried spices

Dried spices have a relatively short life, about 6 months. They are better stored in glass than plastic, and should be kept out of the light.

eggs

Beaten eggs are used in cake making because they entangle air in bubbles and so raise a cake or make it lighter. Eggs also give flavour and colour, and egg yolks enrich a cake mixture. As a precaution, it's advisable to avoid feeding eggs to children under 12 months old to prevent an egg allergy developing; although egg yolks are considered less risky than the whites. It is best for the elderly, very young and others with weakened or compromised immune systems to avoid raw eggs.

Fresh eggs less than 5 days old are best for cooking, and organic and free-range are by far my preference. Look for those that have been kept chilled or stored in a cool environment, and buy from places with a fast turnover of stock. Transfer eggs to the refrigerator as soon as possible. While eggs in a wire basket or bowl may look cute in your kitchen, storing eggs at room temperature hastens their demise – 1 day in a warm kitchen is equal to 4 days in the refrigerator. Eggs have porous shells and should be stored in the cartons they come in, which offer some protection against other food aromas and bacteria. Keep them with the pointed end of the egg facing downwards to help slow moisture loss inside the egg.

If egg whites or yolks are left over from a recipe, they can be stored for other uses. Egg whites will keep for several weeks in the refrigerator, or for several months if frozen. The trick is to remember how many egg whites are in the container! If you forget, you can work it out by measuring the liquid:
- 1 egg white = 30ml = ⅛ cup
- 2 egg whites = 65ml = ¼ cup
- 4 egg whites = 125ml = ½ cup.

Another trick is to weigh them, as the white makes up approximately two-thirds of an egg's weight:
- small (size 5) eggs weigh about 55g (about 35g for the white)
- medium (size 6) eggs weigh about 65g (45g for the white)
- large (size 7) eggs weigh about 75g (50g for the white).

Egg yolks will keep covered and refrigerated for up to 3 days. Spoon a little water over whole egg yolks to stop them forming a skin before covering the bowl with plastic food wrap. Yolks can be frozen for up to a month, but they will then only be good for general cooking jobs, such as acting as a binding agent for meatballs or for glazing pastry. Add a little salt to them before freezing.

flour
For cake making, a soft, low-protein flour milled from soft wheat varieties will produce a cake with a fine, even and tender texture; this is sold as standard flour or cake flour. Low-protein soft flour is also the best for shortcrust pastry and produces a tender, light pastry; but when making choux pastry, use high-grade flour to give the batter strength and structure.

High-grade flour contains more protein and is the one to use when making puff pastry and breads, or in heavier mixtures such as fruit cakes. It is not recommended for general cake making because it will make the crumb tough and cause the cake to 'peak' at the top.

Use self-raising flour as directed; but if not available, use 1¼ teaspoons of baking powder for 160g (1 cup) of standard flour.

frangipane
French; an almond flavoured cream or paste.

ginger preserved in syrup
Also known as stem ginger, this is young ginger that has been preserved in a thick sugar syrup. The ginger can be sliced or chopped and used in cakes, biscuits and puddings, while the syrup is great drizzled over fruit, ice cream or sponge puddings. Once a jar is opened, store in the refrigerator.

golden syrup and treacle
Golden syrup is a by-product of sugar refining – a thick, sticky syrup produced when sugar cane is boiled down to produce sugar. Treacle, produced similarly, is darker and stronger-flavoured. Both syrups are used in baking to give flavour and colour and to help keep baking moist. Golden syrup is sweeter than treacle.

Greek yoghurt
A thick and creamy yoghurt usually made from sheep's milk. If not available, place plain yoghurt in a sieve lined with a piece of paper towel. Drain for 30–60 minutes before carefully turning out into a bowl and peeling off the paper. Beat until smooth.

hazelnuts
Unless hazelnuts are very fresh (see nuts entry), they are best toasted to develop a rich roasted flavour with a mild coffee-like taste. The skins are easily removed after toasting, making the nuts less bitter. To toast hazelnuts, put them in a shallow ovenproof dish and toast in an oven preheated to 180°C for 10–12 minutes, or until you can see the nuts have coloured through the burst skins. Tip nuts onto an old clean cloth, bundle up and rub vigorously to remove skins.

lemons
A lemon tree in the garden is a great asset; just be kind to it. To remove a lemon from the tree, twist the lemon until it pops free – don't pull. If you pull it, a lump of peel can remain on the stalk left on the tree, and this may rot and prevent lemons from growing in the future.

Meyer lemons, with their often bumpy-skinned, large, round, fleshy fruit that have sweetish juice and pith, are not true lemons. They're a hybrid; probably a cross between a lemon and an orange or mandarin.

Cooks love them because they're easy to squeeze and yield plenty of juice; however, they are sweeter than a true lemon, and sometimes do not add enough acidity to a dish. For lemon tarts and dishes that require a more concentrated lemon flavour, I'd use Lisbon lemons if possible – they still have good juice but are more acidic.

Lemons are easier to squeeze when they're at room temperature, but can rot in warm, humid conditions. Keep one or two in the fruit bowl and the rest refrigerated, or leave them on the tree until you need them, or until the end of the season (late spring through to mid-summer depending on the climate). If lemons are very cold, or are not very juicy, roll them several times with the hand to help release the juice, or warm them in a microwave before squeezing.

An average lemon will yield around 1 tablespoon of grated zest and 2½ tablespoons of juice.

limoncello

Sometimes spelled 'lemoncello', this lemon liqueur of Italian origin must be served icy-cold to numb its sweetness. Perhaps at its best poured over perfectly ripe sliced strawberries, it's also good mixed with lightly whipped cream in a sponge sandwich or drizzled over vanilla ice cream and berries. Keep it in the refrigerator and pop it in the freezer 30 minutes before serving.

macaroon

Biscuit made with ground almonds, sugar and egg white.

mango

Aromatic fruit whose flesh is an excellent source of vitamin A. The fleshy parts either side of the large flattish fibrous stone in the centre are called cheeks. Peeling a mango is easily done with a potato peeler. The cheeks can then be cut off as close to the stone as possible, then any additional flesh.

manuka honey

Honey made from the flowers of the manuka tree (native to New Zealand); possesses an earthy, oily, herbaceous aroma and flavour. Rich, dark and intense, it has antibacterial and anti-fungal properties. As a substitute, use an intensely flavoured thick honey. If honey is firm, loosen it in a microwave for a few seconds, or in a small bowl immersed in warm water.

mascarpone

Sometimes described as a cheese, this is actually a thick, rich cream with a high fat content – anything from 50% to 75%! – with a smooth, sticky texture and sweet creamy flavour. It is usually made from cow's milk by adding a culture to the cream, then heating the cream and leaving it to thicken; a good mascarpone is thick enough to support a spoon. It helps thicken mixtures and adds richness, smoothness and a velvety texture.

nuts

It's important to use fresh nuts; old or rancid nuts will mar the flavour of any dish they are added to, and they are difficult to digest; they may even cause stomach upsets. Rancid nuts smell like butter which has been left

for too long at room temperature. Most fresh nuts are creamy coloured, while rancid nuts usually show signs of yellowing. Discard nuts that are showing signs of mould, traces of dirt or insect infestation. Organically grown nuts are generally fresher and worth paying extra for.

Nuts in the shell will keep fresh for up to a year. Whole nuts with their skins on will keep fresher for longer than blanched, sliced, slivered, chopped or ground nuts. Keep nuts in an airtight container away from light in the pantry or in the refrigerator. For longer storage, you can keep them in the freezer; and they don't need thawing before use.

pecans

A relative of the walnut, with a rich, buttery flavour that is a little milder and sweeter than walnut. They can also be toasted, and there is no need to remove the skin as it is not bitter.

quark

A soft, creamy white, fresh curd cheese made from whole, skimmed or semi-skimmed milk. Thicker than Greek yoghurt, with a mild lemony tang, its smooth texture makes it perfect for cheesecakes.

raspberries and blackberries

Raspberries are generally red in colour, although there are deep-red and black fruits, and paler-coloured raspberries, too. They contain more fibre than most other fruits, and 150g (1 cup) of raspberries will provide half your daily vitamin C requirement. And then there's folic acid, manganese, copper and iron. In all, raspberries are an excellent source of antioxidants, especially red and black fruits. Raspberries are fragile, however. Unlike blackberries, which retain their central white core when picked, raspberries are hollow and can easily be squashed. Washing makes them go soft and will dilute their flavour, and if raspberries are stored after washing they will quickly rot. If you must wash them, do so with a minimal amount of water and pat them dry with paper towels, just before they are required. Never soak raspberries or they'll turn into waterlogged blobs.

To keep raspberries and blackberries in pristine condition, transfer them to shallow plastic containers lined with paper towels, cover with more paper towels and keep them in the refrigerator. Berries are infinitely more flavoursome at room temperature, so bring them out of the refrigerator 30 minutes before serving.

ricotta

Although classified as a cheese, ricotta is really a by-product of the cheese-making process – it is made from whey after it has been separated from the curd, and contains only about 13% fat. The whey is heated and the ricotta forms on the surface. The curds and whey have already been heated, so this second heating gives ricotta its name; it means re-cooked.

Ricotta has a delicate milky flavour and should be soft in texture, unlike other curd or cottage cheeses, making it easy to blend with other ingredients. It can be eaten as it is, sweetened with sugar and eaten with fruit, used in sweet dishes, pies, cakes and tortes, and in savoury fillings for pasta dishes and meats.

semolina

A gritty wheat product resulting from milling durum wheat. It is used in pasta, breads and some cakes and biscuits.

sour cream

Has a sharp tang and contains around 20% fat, although lighter products may contain much less than that. It adds lightness, texture and a lemony taste to baking.

strawberries

Strawberries are at their sweetest and best when picked fully ripe; don't pick them early. To store them in pristine condition, line a shallow plastic container with paper towels and put in a layer of strawberries – two layers at most – discarding any imperfect ones as you go. Cover with another piece of paper and keep refrigerated but away from icy areas in the refrigerator. Bring the strawberries to room temperature before serving because chilling mutes their fragrance and flavour.

Washing strawberries dilutes the sweet juice, washes off their intoxicating fragrance and softens their texture, making them flavourless and spongy. On the other hand, they grow close to the earth, and are handled by pickers and packers. The best strawberry is one you pluck fully ripe from the plant at the end of a long, dry day; but whether to wash or not is up to you. Keeping the stems intact until you've washed strawberries can help, and shaking them thoroughly, then patting them dry with paper towels can help a little, too.

sugar
Sugar sweetens cake batters and helps to brown the outside of the cake as it caramelises during baking. It also keeps the texture of the crumb tender.

caster sugar – also called superfine granulated, this is finer than standard granulated sugar and is used in baking because it is easier to cream with butter or mix with other ingredients.

demerara – these hard, light-brown crystals with a mild caramel flavour get their name from Demerara in Guyana. They are especially good for forming a crunchy topping on baking.

granulated sugar – another way to describe regular white sugar (the sort you serve with tea). It's used in syrups because it produces a clearer result than caster sugar, which can produce a cloudy syrup.

icing sugar – also known as confectioner's sugar, this is smooth, fine and powdery. Starch is often added to it to keep it lump-free.

muscovado – a raw sugar with a strong taste of molasses that adds plenty of flavour to rich fruit cakes, boiled fruit cakes and other dried fruit-baking. Pass it through a coarse sieve before using.

soft brown sugar – soft sugar with a sweet caramel flavour.

tamarillos
A subtropical fruit native to South America, but grown extensively in New Zealand. They are ready to eat when soft to the touch; either scoop out the flesh, or peel and slice. To remove the peel, which is bitter, plunge tamarillos into a saucepan of gently boiling water and leave for 15–20 seconds, then drain and cool them quickly in cold water, then peel. They have a sweet, sharp flavour and work well with other sweet fruits, or when sweetened with sugar. An easy way to serve them is to slice and sprinkle with soft brown sugar and leave for a few hours until they give off a crimson juice. Serve with breakfast cereal or ice cream.

vanilla extract
Vanilla essence is a cheap imitation of pure vanilla extract, which is made from vanilla pods.

vanilla pods
These have plenty of flavour and can be reused several times – just as well, as good pods are expensive. After

infusing custards and creams with a vanilla pod, rinse the pod thoroughly under running water. Leave on a piece of paper towel on a sunny windowsill until it is thoroughly dry, then store in a cool dry place in an airtight container. Alternatively, imbed it in a jar of caster sugar and use the flavoured sugar in baking (see also *vanilla sugar*, below).

vanilla sugar
To make, stand a split vanilla pod in a jar of caster sugar with a tight-fitting lid. Leave for at least 3 weeks before using. Alternatively, crush a vanilla pod in a liquidiser with coarse granulated sugar, then store in an airtight container and use as required.

walnuts
Walnuts can be toasted; after toasting, rub them gently to try to remove as much of the skin as possible because it is bitter-tasting. See also *nuts* entry.

weights and measures

For baking, it pays to invest in a measuring scale. Look for one with increments of 1g (not 5g), to ensure accuracy – which is important in baking.

Buy metal measuring spoons and glass measuring jugs (not plastic ones), because they will hold their shape forever and provide accurate measuring. Try to find jugs with lots of increment markings on the side, again for accuracy.

If you don't have scales, the following charts include conversions from spoon and cup measures to weights.

grams to ounces and vice versa

GENERAL			EXACT		
30g	=	1oz	1oz	=	28.35g
60g	=	2oz	2oz	=	56.70g
90g	=	3oz	3oz	=	85.05g
120g	=	4oz	4oz	=	113.04g
150g	=	5oz	5oz	=	141.08g
180g	=	6oz	6oz	=	170.01g
210g	=	7oz	7oz	=	198.04g
230g	=	8oz	8oz	=	226.08g
260g	=	9oz	9oz	=	255.01g
290g	=	10oz	10oz	=	283.05g
320g	=	11oz	11oz	=	311.08g
350g	=	12oz	12oz	=	340.02g
380g	=	13oz	13oz	=	368.05g
410g	=	14oz	14oz	=	396.09g
440g	=	15oz	15oz	=	425.02g
470g	=	16oz	16oz	=	453.06g

Recipes are based on the rounded gram values in the 'general' column.

liquid measurements

25ml	(28.4ml)	=	1fl oz					
150ml	(142ml)	=	5fl oz	=	¼ pint	=	1 gill
275ml	(284ml)	=	10fl oz	=	½ pint		
425ml	(426ml)	=	15fl oz	=	¾ pint		
575ml	(568ml)	=	20fl oz	=	1 pint (imperial)		

Note:

450ml	(454ml)	=	16fl oz	=	1 pint (USA)

spoon measures

¼ teaspoon	=	1.25ml
½ teaspoon	=	2.5ml
1 teaspoon	=	5ml
1 tablespoon	=	15ml

Note:
In NZ, SA, USA and UK 1 tablespoon = 15ml
In Australia 1 tablespoon = 20ml
1 tablespoon butter = about 10g

cup measures for liquids

⅛ cup	=	30ml
¼ cup	=	65ml
⅓ cup	=	85ml
½ cup	=	125ml
⅔ cup	=	170ml
¾ cup	=	190ml
1 cup	=	250ml

baking tin sizes

15cm	=	6in
18cm	=	7in
20cm	=	8in
23cm	=	9in
25.5cm	=	10in
28cm	=	11in
30.5cm	=	12in

cup measures for 'dry' ingredients

FLOURS AND SUGARS	¼ CUP	⅓ CUP	½ CUP	1 CUP
cornflour	35g	50g	70g	140g
standard/self-raising/high-grade flour	35g	45g	70g	140g
caster sugar	55g	75g	110g	220g
granulated	55g	75g	110g	220g
demerara sugar	55g	75g	105g	210g
icing sugar	40g	55g	80g	160g
light/soft brown sugar (lightly packed)	40g	55g	80g	160g
muscovado sugar (light)	25g	50g	75g	150g

OTHER INGREDIENTS	¼ CUP	⅓ CUP	½ CUP	1 CUP
almonds, ground	30g	40g	60g	120g
almonds, blanched (whole)	40g	55g	80g	160g
almonds, slivered	35g	50g	70g	140g
amaretti biscuits	30g	40g	60g	120g
apricots, dried (whole)	45g	55g	85g	170g
blackberries, raspberries	25g	50g	75g	150g
breadcrumbs, fresh white	15g	20g	30g	60g
currants	35g	50g	70g	140g
fruit mince	80g	105g	160g	320g
hazelnuts, whole	30g	40g	60g	120g
mascarpone	50g	70g	100g	200g
medium-grain rice	55g	75g	110g	220g
oats, wholegrain	30g	40g	60g	120g
pecans, halves	30g	40g	55g	110g
quark	60g	80g	120g	240g
ricotta	50g	70g	100g	200g
semolina (fine)	45g	60g	90g	180g
sultanas	40g	55g	80g	160g
walnuts, halves	25g	35g	50g	100g
walnuts, pieces	30g	40g	60g	120g

Note: cup measures for dry ingredients are rounded to the nearest 5g.

measurements

cm to approx inches

0.5cm	=	¼in	5cm	=	2in
1.25cm	=	½in	7.5cm	=	3in
2.5cm	=	1in	10cm	=	4in

oven temperatures

CELSIUS	FAHRENHEIT	GAS	
110°C	225°F	¼	very cool
120°C	250°F	½	
140°C	275°F	1	cool
150°C	300°F	2	
170°C	325°F	3	moderate
180°C	350°F	4	
190°C	375°F	5	moderately hot
200°C	400°F	6	
220°C	425°F	7	hot
230°C	450°F	8	
240°C	475°F	9	very hot

abbreviations

g	gram
kg	kilogram
mm	millimetre
cm	centimetre
ml	millilitre
tsp	teaspoon
Tbsp	tablespoon
°C	degrees Celsius
°F	degrees Fahrenheit
in	inch
lb	pound
oz	ounce
fl oz	fluid ounce

index